CICERO'S ETHICAL VISION

AN INTRODUCTION TO CICERO'S MORAL PHILOSOPHY

MICHAEL A. SCHINTGEN

Wasteland Press
www.wastelandpress.net
Shelbyville, KY USA

Cicero's Ethical Vision:
An Introduction to Cicero's Moral Philosophy
by Michael A. Schintgen

Copyright © 2021 Michael A. Schintgen
ALL RIGHTS RESERVED

First Printing – September 2021
Paperback ISBN: 978-1-68111-432-3

NO PART OF THIS BOOK MAY BE REPRODUCED IN ANY
FORM, BY PHOTOCOPYING OR BY ANY ELECTRONIC OR
MECHANICAL MEANS, INCLUDING INFORMATION
STORAGE OR RETRIEVAL SYSTEMS, WITHOUT PERMISSION
IN WRITING FROM THE COPYRIGHT OWNER/AUTHOR

Printed in the U.S.A.

0   1   2   3   4

TABLE OF CONTENTS

CHAPTER I
Cicero the Philosopher?

Marcus Tullius Cicero (106-43 BCE) ranks as one of history's greatest orators. His Latin works were staples of the Western schoolboy diet into the early twentieth century.[1] Yet, starting in the 19th century, one substantial body of his writings has come to be largely neglected. These are his philosophical writings. Why did Cicero come to not be taken seriously as a philosopher? The common view is shaped by negative writers of the 19th and 20th centuries, and may be summarized under four headings.[2]

---

[1] For a biography of Cicero, see Anthony Everitt, *Cicero: The Life and Times of Rome's Greatest Politician* (New York: Random House, 2001). A brief overview of Cicero's philosophical background and works is available online in the Internet Encyclopedia of Philosophy article on Cicero: http://www.iep.utm.edu/cicero/ [accessed May 10, 2021]

[2] For discussions of the cause and development of negative views of Cicero's philosophical status, see Neal Wood, *Cicero's Social and Political Thought* (Berkeley: U of California Press, 1988), 6-13; Timothy W. Caspar, *Recovering the Ancient View of Founding: A Commentary on Cicero's De Legibus* (Lanham, MD: Rowman & Littlefield, 2011), 5-8; and Walter Nicgorski, "Cicero and the Rebirth of Political Philosophy," *Political Science Reviewer* 8 (1978): 73-81, Reprinted in *Cicero's Practical Philosophy*, ed. Walter Nicgorski (South Bend, Ind: University of Notre Dame Press, 2012), 251-259.

First, Cicero came to be viewed as a copyist rather than as an original philosopher. Hence, it was thought, he may be a useful source for studying the history of philosophy, but is not himself of philosophical interest.

Second, he came to be labelled an Eclectic, whose works are mere patchworks of earlier ideas, lacking any rigorous connection, and hence unworthy of serious study.

Third, his avowed skepticism seemed to disqualify him as a constructive philosopher. His work could at best be negative, critiquing other positions, but never developing one of his own. Skeptical arguments can be found anywhere, one might say; why dredge up those from 2,000 years ago?

Fourth, and perhaps most devastatingly, Cicero acquired the reputation of not being sincere and honest in his philosophical arguments. His works were dismissed as mere propaganda to bolster socially useful beliefs that lack rigor or coherence. On this view, Cicero does not really argue because he is not really interested in truth. Thus, Cicero seems irrelevant to those seeking truth.

Although a full response can only be accomplished in an unfolding of Cicero's philosophy in later chapters, we will briefly examine each criticism in turn.

Cicero the Copyist

Referring to one of Cicero's works, Arthur Stanley Pease once remarked that "modern study of the [*On the Nature of the Gods*] has been rather more concerned with the detection of its sources than with interpretation of its contents and its purpose."[3] This is understandable. Cicero's dialogues present us with a patchwork of material, and often the seams are showing. Because of this, Cicero's philosophical works are often treated as sourcebooks in which to discover clues as to the positions of philosophers whose works are otherwise lost.[4] J. Jackson Barlow notes that:

> The prevailing scholarly view of Cicero's teaching holds that his philosophic works are primarily derivative from several other schools of Greek philosophy current in his day. They are regarded as valuable chiefly for the insights they provide into the teachings of others, as for example the Stoic philosopher Panaetius, whose own works are now lost. Cicero's achievement consists in the arrangement and presentation of the thought of others, not in his originality as a philosopher.[5]

This approach may be useful for the historian of philosophy, but if this is all there is to Cicero's philosophical writings, they would seem to hold little claim to be regarded as truly *philosophical* works. Is this in fact the case? Let us see what evidence this view of Cicero is based on.

---

[3] Arthur Stanley Pease, introduction, vol. 1, *De Natura Deorum* (Cambridge: Cambridge UP, 1955-58), 36.

[4] David T. Runia gives a table displaying the paucity of the extant works of ancient philosophers as an appendix to his chapter "Aristotle and Theophrastus Conjoined in the Writings of Cicero" found in *Cicero's Knowledge of the Peripatos*, ed. W. W. Fortenhaugh and P. Steinmetz (Edison, N.J: Transcation Publishers, 1989), 35-36.

[5] J. Jackson Barlow, "The Education of Statesmen in Cicero's *De Republica*," *Polity* (Spring, 1987): 354. For a criticism of Cicero's originality, see J. C. Davies, "The Originality of Cicero's Philosophical Works," *Latomus*. (Jan-Mar, 1971): 105-119.

Much has been made of Cicero's comment in a letter to his friend Atticus regarding some writings he was producing that "they are copies, involving little labor, I merely supply the words, of which I have an abundance."[6] Curiously, for all the negative judgements that are made from these lines, the letter does not explicitly refer to his philosophical writings. In fact, no context or reference is given at all. As the only substantial writing he is known to have been engaged in at the time was his philosophical series, the application of this passage seems reasonable if not certain.[7] Nevertheless, as we shall see, Cicero is undoubtedly being overly deprecatory of his own works.[8]

Furthermore, there also appears to be an overlooking of the different character of his various philosophical writings. In his later series of dialogues, he very deliberately was trying to keep his own views in the background and present the prominent philosophical positions of his day. There is no need to apply this same purpose to the earlier *On the Republic* and *On the Laws*, where he does explicitly state that he is doing more than copying his sources. He explains that "it is very easy to translate another man's ideas, and I might do that, *if I did not fully*

---

[6] *Ad Atticum* 12.52. Translation from Cicero, *On Obligations*, trans. P. G. Walsh (Oxford: Oxford UP, 2000), 129.

[7] Walsh suggests the reference is to Cicero's more technical *Academica*: Walsh 129. For further discussion see J. G. F. Powell, "Introduction: Cicero's Philosophical Works and their Background," in *Cicero the Philosopher: Twelve Papers* (Oxford: Oxford UP, 1995), 8-9n20; A. E.; Douglas, "Cicero the Philosopher." *Cicero*. Ed. T. A. Dorey London: Routledge & Keegan Paul, 1964), 138-139; and Nicgorski, *Rebirth* 73, *Practical Philosophy* 252.

[8] G. F. Poyser, Introduction, *Cicero: De Re Publica*, trans G. F. Poyser (Cambridge, MA: Cambridge UP, 1948), 11-12.

wish to be myself. For what difficulty is there in presenting the same thoughts rendered in practically the same phrases?" [emphasis added][9]

Nor should his disclaimer be automatically applied to his last work, *On Duties*, which stands apart from the series and is addressed in Cicero's own name to his son. In fact, in *On Duties* he makes a point of declaring he is doing more than merely copying from his sources, in this case the Stoic philosopher Panaetius. He states that "I shall, therefore, at this time and in this investigation follow chiefly the Stoics, not as translator, but, as is my custom, I shall at my own option and discretion draw from those sources in such measure and in such manner as shall suit my purpose."[10]

Cicero the Eclectic

Closely connected to the view that Cicero is only a copyist is that he takes ideas indiscriminately from whatever sources he finds appealing, and hence is labelled an Eclectic. This term has a negative connotation, suggesting one takes haphazardly what one likes from earlier philosophers without any internal consistency.

Cicero readily admits and boasts of his independence from any one school of philosophy. As he declares in the *Tusculan Disputations*, "let everyone defend his views, for judgement is free: I shall cling to my rule and without being tied to the laws of any single school of thought which I feel bound to obey, shall always search for the most probable solution to

---

[9] *On the Laws* 2.17. Cicero, *On the Republic and On the Laws*, trans. C. W. Keyes, The Loeb Classical Library 213 (Cambridge, MA: Harvard UP, 1928), 391. Unless otherwise noted, all translations of *On the Laws* will be from this translation.

[10] *On Duties* 1.6. Cicero, *On Duties*, trans. Walter Miller, The Loeb Classical Library 30 (Cambridge, MA: Harvard UP, 1913), 9.

every problem."[11] He is thus willing to take arguments from whatever source seems to him most probable. It would be difficult if not impossible to find a philosopher who does not owe a debt to his predecessors. For Cicero, examining the positions of the various philosophical schools is a means of arriving at truth. He proclaims in *On the Nature of the Gods* that "if it is a considerable matter to understand any one of the systems of philosophy singly, how much harder is it to master them all! Yet this is the task that confronts those whose principle is to discover the truth by the method of arguing both for and against all the schools.[12]

Cicero does indicate which philosophers he finds most worthwhile: Plato, Aristotle, and the Stoics.[13] And he will give reasons at various points for taking arguments from one or the other source. But, philosophically speaking, the important issue is whether or not his positions, whatever their sources, are rationally defensible and logically consistent. Explaining how Cicero does in fact develop such an ethical philosophy will be the goal of this book.

Cicero the Skeptic

Cicero is quite open in his preference for the Skeptical approach in philosophy. However, his position is often misunderstood. To

---

[11] *Tusculan Disputations* 4.7. Cicero, *Tusculan Disputations*, trans. J. E. King, The Loeb Classical Library 141 (Cambridge, MA: Harvard UP, 1927), 335. Unless otherwise noted, all translations of the *Tusculan Disputations* will be from this translation.

[12] *On the Nature of the Gods* 1.11. Cicero, *Nature of the Gods and Academics*, trans. H. Rackham, The Loeb Classical Library 268 (Cambridge, MA: Harvard UP, 1933), 15. Unless otherwise noted, all translations of *The Nature of the Gods* will be from this translation.

[13] See *On the Laws* 3.1; *Tusculan Disputations* 3.22; *On Duties* 1.2, 5-6.

modern ears, skepticism suggests thoroughgoing doubt, along the lines of Descartes' "I took to be virtually false everything that was merely probable."[14] Cicero's approach is rather that of Plato's *Timaeus* (which he partially translated) where the titular character seeks for the most probable account of the origin of the universe even though certainty will be impossible:

> Don't therefore be surprised, Socrates, if on many matters concerning the gods and the whole world of change we are unable in every respect and on every occasion to render consistent and accurate account. You must be satisfied if our account is as likely as any, remembering that both I and you who are sitting in judgement on it are merely human, and should not look for anything more than a likely story in such matters. [15]

Timaeus' position does not preclude, but rather affirms that one can have good reasons for maintaining one position against others. Similarly, Cicero's skeptical position does not necessitate that he takes a wholly negative and destructive attitude. Cicero explains his purpose in the introduction to his *On the Nature of the Gods*:

> Our position is not that we hold that nothing is true, but that we assert that all true sensations are associated with false ones so closely resembling them that they contain no infallible mark to guide our judgment and assent. From this followed the corollary, that many sensations are *probable*, that is, though not

---

[14] Rene Descartes, *Discourse on Method*, trans. Donald A. Cress (Indianapolis: Hackett, 1980), 5.

[15] *Timaeus* 29c. Plato, *Timaeus*, trans. Desmond Lee. (New York: Penguin, 1965), 42. For Cicero's translation see *Ricerche Sul Testo Del Timeo Ciceroniano*, ed. Remo Giomini (Rome: Angelo Signorelli, 1967).

amounting to full perception they are yet possessed of a certain distinctness and clearness, and so can serve to direct the conduct of the wise man.[16]

In Cicero's view, accepting the probable is not opposed to the seeking truth. Rather, the probable is often the farthest one can advance towards knowing the truth about reality. The question of interest will be, on what grounds does he consider some arguments to be more probable than others?[17]

Cicero the Propagandist

Finally, what are we to make of claim that Cicero is a mere promoter of socially useful views that he might not have even truly believed in himself? This position asserts that Cicero writes to promote virtues that maintained Roman society, but does not believe them to be true or at least provable. In this context, reference is often made to the first book of the *On the Laws*, where Cicero explains that:

> Our whole discourse is intended to promote the firm foundation of States, the strengthening of cities, and the curing of the ills of peoples. For that reason I want to be especially careful not to lay down first principles that have not been wisely considered and thoroughly investigated. Of course I

---

[16] *The Nature of the Gods* 1.12.

[17] On the meaning of skepticism in Cicero See A. A. Long, "Cicero's Plato and Aristotle," *Cicero the Philosopher: Twelve Papers*, ed. J. G. F. Powel (Oxford: Oxford UP, 1995), 41-42; Nicgorski, *Rebirth*, 67-68, *Practical*, 246-247 and his *Cicero's Skepticism and His Recovery of Political Philosophy* (New York: Palgrave MacMillan, 2016); Raphael Woolf, *Cicero: The Philosophy of a Roman Sceptic* (New York: Routledge, 2015); John Wynne, "Cicero," *Skepticism: From Antiquity to the Present*, ed. Diego Machuca and Baron Reed (New York: Bloomsbury, 2019), 93-101.

cannot expect that they will be universally accepted, for that is impossible; but I do look for the approval of all who believe that everything which is right and honourable is to be desired for its own sake, and that nothing whatever is to be accounted a good unless it is praiseworthy in itself, or at least nothing should be considered a great good unless it can rightly be praised for its own sake.[18]

A criticism of this position is offered by James E. Holton. He claims that Cicero's position is contradictory because "the fundamentally Stoic teaching which he propounds as his own in the *Laws* rests in part on an understanding of divine providence and an anthropocentric teleology which he himself had examined and rejected in two other works—*On the Nature of the Gods* and *On Divination*."[19]

The relationship between the views presented in the two works that Holton names here and Cicero's central claims about the foundation for natural law will need to be examined in their proper place. At this stage, what is of interest is Holton's interpretation of how this perceived discrepancy is to be explained:

It is reasonable to suggest that this apparent inconsistency has its roots in the fact that the teaching in the *Laws* is addressed not to philosophers but primarily to all decent and honourable men. The immediate task is a practical one: "to promote the

---

[18] *On the Laws* 1.37.

[19] James E. Holton, "Marcus Tullius Cicero," in *History of Political Philosophy 3rd ed.*, ed. Leo Strauss and Joseph Cropsey (Chicago: University of Chicago Press), 171. See Leo Strauss, *Natural Right and History* (Chicago: University of Chicago Press, 1968), 155-156.

firm foundation of states, the strengthening of cities, and the curing of the ills of peoples."[20]

One is left puzzling as to whether Cicero is merely playing a game with his readers. If Cicero has, according to Holton, rejected the prerequisites for natural law, is there then any foundation for his presentation of natural law to the non-philosophic? If Cicero is aware of this inconsistency, he seems to be foisting empty claims on a gullible audience. If he is not aware of an inconsistency, he must be a muddled and careless thinker. In either case, the value of studying his works would seem to be minimal.

Cicero's personal beliefs and psychological condition are not discoverable with certainty. Nor are they per se the concern of a philosophical study. A philosopher as philosopher can only examine the arguments presented in a work and evaluate whether they are valid or invalid, coherent or incoherent. One would expect, however, that the more compelling and consistent a philosopher's arguments are, the more likely he or she is to actually hold them. On the other hand, sloppiness and inconsistency will suggest a lack of seriousness or personal acceptance of the theses presented. A definite conclusion regarding these issues will only be possible following the careful examination of what Cicero actually wrote in the following chapters.

---

[20] Holton, 171. The quotation is from Cicero's *On the Laws* 1.37.

Is there a Distinctly Ciceronian Moral Philosophy?

Although interest in Cicero's philosophical writings has increased in recent years, [21] there is still relatively little study of them as truly *philosophical* works. One may find much philological discussion, or investigations of the sources Cicero made use of, or even sociological studies of Cicero and his time. But little can be found that treats his writings in the manner one expects of studies of a work of philosophy. Treatments of Cicero's philosophical corpus often resemble literary criticism rather than philosophical studies. The resulting impression is that his works are not worthy of, or would not stand up to, the sort of analysis one would give to a work of Aristotle or Kant. Furthermore, the study of Cicero's philosophical views seems to have remained within the domain of classicists and, to a lesser extent, political scientists, rather than philosophers.

In contrast with the still common view, the present study represents an attempt to take Cicero seriously as a philosopher. Concretely, this means not focusing exclusively on his conclusions, but investigating and clarifying his premises and the arguments he makes from these to reach his conclusions. This seems like the typical treatment one would expect a philosopher to receive, but Cicero's philosophical works rarely receive such consideration in recent times.

To what extent can Cicero be said to have a distinct, individual philosophy? This question is complicated by his use of the dialogue form. In several dialogues, Cicero himself appears as a speaker. One wonders how far one should take the statements of Cicero the character

---

[21] J. G. F. Powell traces this renewed interest to the early 1980s in: "Introduction: Cicero's Philosophical Works and their Background," in *Cicero the Philosopher: Twelve Papers* (Oxford: Oxford UP, 1995), 1-2.

to be identical with the conclusion of Cicero the author.[22] Only his last philosophical work, *On Duties*, is presented unambiguously in his own name, offering guidance to his son Marcus. Thus, a strong case could be made for giving the greatest weight to the *On Duties*. But *On Duties* has a special audience in view and leaves much background unexplained. How do his other philosophical works fit into the picture?

Cicero's philosophical corpus can be considered as forming three, generally chronological, categories:[23]

I)   The works of the mid to early 50's BCE: *On the Republic* and *On the Laws*

II)   The Philosophical Series of 45-44 BCE: *Hortensius, Academics, On Ends, Tusculan Disputations, On the Nature of the Gods, On Divination, On Fate.*[24]
      Outside of this series, though written in the same period are *On Consolation, On Old Age, Laelius,* and *Cato.*[25]

III) *On Duties* (44 BCE)

---

[22] Cicero is a character in *On the Laws, Academics, On Ends, On the Nature of the Gods, On Divination* and *On Fate*. He may perhaps appear in the *Tusculan Disputations*, but this is unclear. One of the speakers is identified only as M. This could mean Magister (teacher), or could stand for Marcus. See J. E. King, preface to *Tusculan Disputations*, The Loeb Classical Library 141 (Cambridge, MA: Harvard UP, 1927), 10-11 n.2.

[23] A detailed chronological chart may be found in Powell xiii-xvii.

[24] This plan is discussed in *On Divination* 2.1-4. Only two (from different editions) of the proposed four books of *Academics* are extant. *Hortensius, On Fate,* and *Cato* only exist in fragments.

[25] *On Divination* 2.3.

This book will not attempt to analyze Cicero's philosophy in all branches, but only his ethical philosophy. The early works (*On the Republic* and *On the Laws*) represent an initial articulation of his ethical and political views. The works in the Philosophical Series of 45-44 BCE present a synopsis of conflicting views, according to Cicero (speaking of *On Ends*), "in such a way that the conflicting views of the different philosophers might be known" on the major areas of philosophy.[26] Cicero himself warns the reader not to be too keen to discover his own personal views in them because he has a specific pedagogical purpose in mind:

> Those however who seek to learn my personal opinion on the various questions show an unreasonable degree of curiosity. In discussion it is not so much weight of authority as force of arguments that should be demanded. Indeed the authority of those who profess to teach is often a positive hindrance to those who desire to learn; they cease to employ their own judgement, and take what they perceive to be the verdict of their chosen master as settling the question.[27]

Nevertheless, certain parts of the discussions may shed light on points made elsewhere. Finally, *On Duties* presents us with Cicero's last word on ethics, and thus is the final articulation of the position first set out in *On the Republic* and *On the Laws*.

---

[26] *On Divination* 2.2. Cicero, *On Old Age, On Friendship, On Divination*, trans. William Armistead Falconer, The Loeb Classical Library 154 (Cambridge, MA: Harvard UP, 1923), 371. All translations of the *On Divination* will be from this translation.

[27] *On the Nature of the Gods* 1.10.

Prelude to Cicero's Ethics

If there is a specifically Ciceronian ethical teaching, what are its chief characteristics? Perhaps a useful entry point is the introduction to his earliest philosophical work, the *On the Republic*. In his introduction, Cicero quotes with approval a saying he attributes to the Greek Philosopher Xenocrates.[28] When asked what advantage is to be obtained from his teaching, he responds that his disciples learned "to do of their own accord what they are compelled to do by the law."[29] Besides the obvious emphasis Cicero gives to the practical application of philosophical knowledge, the contrast between one's own accord and the compulsion of law is striking. Cicero's approval of this statement suggests that he considers one of the main tasks of the philosopher to be to reveal a congruence between what one should choose freely and (at least some) laws. That is to say, the laws of society can be something more than an imposition forcing the individual to do what he does not want to do. Taking law here to refer to just laws, one can ask what is the connection between the individual good and the requirements of justice, and hence obeying just laws?

A further puzzle arises from another of Cicero's favorite quotations, this time from Socrates. In his *On the Laws* Cicero refers to a statement attributed to Socrates that he was right to "curse the

---

[28] Diogenes Laertius attributes this statement to Aristotle. DL 5.20. See Diogenes Laertius, *Lives of Eminent Philosophers*, trans. R. D. Hicks, The Loeb Classical Library 184 (Cambridge, MA: Harvard UP, 1972), 468.

[29] *Republic* 1.3, Cicero, *On the Republic and On the Laws*, trans. C. W. Keyes, The Loeb Classical Library 213 (Cambridge, MA: Harvard UP, 1928), 17. Unless otherwise noted, all translations of the *Republic* will be from this translation.

man who first separated self-interest from justice."[30] The connection between self-interest and justice will be a key to understanding Cicero's ethical philosophy. It reaches its fullest articulation in *On Duties*, where the link between utility and justice will be found in the noble or honorable.

The analysis of Cicero's position will unfold in the following way. Chapter 2 will offer a preliminary treatment of the key themes of justice and natural law as presented by the character Laelius in Cicero's *On the Republic* Book 3. The following chapter (chapter 3) will investigate Cicero's natural law position as found in his *On the Laws, On Ends*, and *On Duties*. In order to clarify Cicero's position, chapter 4 will compare his version of natural law to the positions of Thomas Aquinas and Immanuel Kant. The fifth chapter will examine Cicero's treatment of the motivation for acting morally by means of an analysis of the *Dream of Scipio* found at the end of his *On the Republic*. Chapter 6 will consider the role of the honorable and obligations in the first book of *On Duties*. Finally, the seventh chapter will consider Cicero's reconciliation of the honorable and the useful in *On Duties* Books 2 and 3.

---

[30] *On the Laws* 1.33. See *On Duties* 2.11.

CHAPTER II
Preliminary Consideration: Laelius's Defense of Justice in On the Republic 3

Where does one begin an investigation of Cicero's ethical theory? One is handicapped by Cicero's decision to write in dialogue form. He wrote no definitive treatise on ethics, or any other philosophical topic. Rather, his ideas are often found woven into a collection of dialogues. For several reasons, this book will begin with a consideration of his earliest philosophical dialogues, *On the Republic* and *On the Laws*. Given that these are Cicero's first philosophical dialogues, it seems reasonable to take these as the starting point of inquiry. Secondly, as will be shown, the *On the Republic* and *On the Laws* contain discussions of what Cicero takes to be the fundamental issues of ethics. Therefore, an examination of these works will provide an orientation to Cicero's ethical vision. Finally, the central themes of *On the Republic* and *On the Laws* will be developed more fully in Cicero's final work *On Duties*. Thus, an examination of these earlier works will provide background necessary for understanding and appreciating Cicero's most mature ethical thought.

Cicero's *On the Republic* and Plato's *Republic*

As the title of the work suggests, Cicero wrote his *On the Republic* in conscious response to Plato's *Republic*.[31] Although he took Plato's work as his point of departure, he developed his own vision of ethics. In particular, Cicero places great emphasis on discovering the nature of justice. Unfortunately, *On the Republic* exists in an incomplete condition. What remains, however, will be sufficient for our present purpose—developing an initial orientation to Cicero's treatment of justice.[32]

Defining justice is, at first glance, fairly straightforward. In the second book of *On the Republic*, Cicero makes use of what is now the standard textbook definition, stating that justice means "to give everyone that which is his due."[33] This usage links Cicero's work back to that of Plato, for this definition is given in the *Republic*.[34] However, the apparent straightforwardness of the meaning of justice is illusory. The basic definition of justice is not, in the abstract, controversial. What it means concretely is a source of dispute. For what, precisely, is

---

[31] In fact, the title *Republic* for the work of Plato was given by Cicero. The Greek title is *Politeia*. For discussions of the relationship between Plato's *Republic* and Cicero's *Republic*, See MacKendrick, 55; and *On the Commonwealth and On the Laws*, trans. James E. G. Zetzel, Cambridge Texts in the History of Philosophy (Cambridge: Cambridge UP, 1999), xiii-xiv.

[32] The major surviving portions are from books 1-3, recovered in 1820, and the end of book 6 which is the famous *Dream of Scipio*. See Zetzel, xiv-xv.

[33] *On the Republic* 3.19.

[34] *Republic* 1.331e, where it is attributed to the poet Simonides.

due to another? One will find agreement among philosophers and the public at large that justice is to give to someone what is due to them, but great disagreement as to what exactly *is* due. Contemporary debates often hinge upon, and are often irresolvable because of, different ideas of what is due.[35]

To understand how Cicero both follows and departs from Plato, a brief consideration of the discussion about the nature of justice in the first two books of Plato's *Republic* will be helpful. The issues and challenges presented at the beginning of Plato's *Republic* are also those taken up by Cicero in his own *On the Republic*. Book 1 of the *On the Republic* serves as a prologue to the rest of the dialogue by raising difficulties about what justice is.[36] Socrates first questions Cephalus. After a brief conversation, it emerges that Cephalus understands that the essence of justice consists in fulfilling one's legal and business debts.[37] But Socrates presents Cephalus with a challenge to his view of justice:

> But as to this very thing, justice, shall we so simply assert that it is the truth and giving back what a man has taken from another, or is to do these very things sometimes just and sometimes unjust? Take this case as an example of what I mean: everyone would surely say that if a man takes weapons from a friend when the latter is of sound mind, and the friend demands them back when he is mad, one shouldn't give back such things, and the man who gave them back would not be

---

[35] See "Justice as a Virtue: Changing Conceptions" in Alasdair MacIntyre, *After Virtue* (Notre Dame: University of Notre Dame Press, 1981), 244-255.

[36] It has been argued that *Republic* 1 was originally a freestanding dialogue to which the other books were later added. See Gregory Vlastos, *Socrates: Ironist and Moral Philosopher* (Cambridge: Cambridge UP, 1991), 46-47.

[37] *Republic* 1.331a-c.

just, and moreover, one should not be willing to tell someone in this state the whole truth.[38]

These questions put Cephalus in a quandary. By his earlier comments about justice, he would seem compelled to affirm that you should return the weapon to your insane friend. But this does not sound quite right. On the other hand, if he agrees that the weapon should not be returned, he will be forced to abandon his straightforward view of justice and seek a more adequate and complex understanding. Coming to such an understanding would require Cephalus to seek for a natural or metaphysical basis for justice, not merely a legal or contractual basis. Seen in such a light, some of Cephalus' actions might be revealed to be not truly just. He escapes this dilemma by quickly leaving the scene, passing on the argument to his son Polemarchus.

Polemarchus will posit that what is due to another means "doing good to friends and harm to enemies."[39] Socrates' exchange with him takes many twists and turns, but a few major points should be noted. Polemarchus' definition hinges on two sets of interrelated terms: good/bad and friends/enemies. Like his father, he does not recognize that his own assumptions are open to challenge. For Polemarchus, as he tells Socrates, the essence of justice is the securing of partnerships for the acquiring of wealth.[40] Friends are those who are helpful in these pursuits. But Socrates questions his understanding of friendship when

---

[38] *Republic* 1.331c. From Plato, *The Republic*, trans. Allan Bloom (New York: Basic Books, 1968), 7. All quotations from Plato's *Republic* will be from this translation.

[39] *Republic* 1.332d.

[40] *Republic* 1.333a.

he asks, "Do you mean by friends those who seem to be good to an individual, or those who are, even if they don't seem to be, and similarly with enemies?"[41] Furthermore, "Is it...the part of a just man to injure any human being whatsoever?"[42] Socrates' questioning revolves around attempting to discover what is truly good and what true friendship consists in.

The final definition in *Republic* 1 is proffered by the sophist Thrasymachus, who holds that justice is simply "the advantage of the stronger,"[43] i.e., the advantage of those in power. Justice thus is not founded upon metaphysical principles, but is simply a term used to describe what will profit the ruler or rulers. Injustice means acting for one's own advantage rather than that of the ruler. A private citizen is only "just" because of fear of punishment. Socrates eventually silences Thrasymachus, but several of the other participants in the dialogue (particularly Glaucon and Adeimantus[44]) are not satisfied that Socrates has actually refuted his position. Hence what justice positively means remains elusive.

In fact, the discussion of justice in Book 1 of the *Republic* is really only a prelude to a more radical questioning in the remaining books. This questioning is initiated in Book 2 by Glaucon in his famous story of the Ring of Gyges. In this story, the shepherd Gyges finds a magic ring that allows him to become invisible. He uses it to assassinate his

---

[41] *Republic* 1.334c.

[42] *Republic* 1.335b.

[43] *Republic* 1.338c.

[44] Glaucon and Adeimantus are both brothers of Plato.

king and take his place.[45] By means of this story, Glaucon wishes to spur Socrates to provide an explanation as to why justice is intrinsically desirable. People seem to praise justice, Glaucon claims, not for itself, but for the advantages that follow from it. On the other hand, injustice is avoided because one will be punished if one is caught performing unjust actions. But what if one could be unjust and not get caught? Why should one not do so if it would be to one's own advantage? Why should I follow justice rather than my own advantage? Glaucon's challenge becomes the springboard for the discussions in the rest of the *On the Republic*. It is also, we shall see, the challenge Cicero will take up in his *On the Republic*.

From this consideration of *Republic* 1, two important questions about justice emerge:

1) What does it mean to be just?
2) Why should I be just rather than unjust?

These will be the chief issues for Cicero in his *On the Republic*.

Cicero and the Question of Justice

Although Cicero takes Plato as his inspiration, his *On the Republic* differs in important ways from Plato's *Republic*. The opening conversation in Book 1 of Plato's work involves private citizens discussing the nature of justice. Cicero, after his introduction, begins with a discussion of justice dominated by Scipio Aemilianus, hero of the Third Punic War and prominent statesman. Whereas Plato is

---

[45] *Republic* 2.359c-368c.

initially concerned with justice for an individual, Cicero's characters' initial interest is in discovering a just form of society. Plato, in the second through fifth books of his *Republic*, creates an idealized society in order to discover the nature of justice. In the second book of *On the Republic*, Scipio narrates the history of Rome to see how an actually existing just state has come into being.

Cicero has Scipio contrast the two approaches. He claims that "[Plato]...has sought for and has created a State of a kind that is to be desired rather than hoped for—one of the smallest size, not such as to be actually possible, but in which it might be possible to see the workings of his theory of the State."[46] Plato, Scipio emphasizes, is motivated by theoretical rather than practical considerations. Plato's proposed city is not considered by Scipio to be a viable political institution. Scipio and his friends are not interested in abstract speculation, but in what might actually be achievable. Thus, he explains:

> As for me, however, I shall endeavour, if I am able to accomplish my purpose, employing the same principles which Plato discerned, yet taking no shadowy commonwealth of the imagination, but a real and very powerful State, to seem to you to be pointing out, as with a demonstrating rod, the causes of every political good and ill.[47]

Intriguingly, Scipio indicates that the discussion in which he and his associates are about to engage will be making use of the same principles as Plato made use of in his very different work. As the

---

[46] *On the Republic* 2.52.

[47] *On the Republic* 2.52.

discussion unfolds, these principles are seen to include justice, the good, the nature of the soul, and the requirements for communal life. However, to this similarity of principles will be added an additional principle, that the discussion be guided by an understanding of what is possible. And what is possible will largely be judged as that which is actually in existence, the Roman Republic itself. Cicero's point is that a real understanding of the nature of justice is best discovered by considering historical realities rather than an imaginary and highly unreliable ideal. Plato's procedure, Cicero seems to be suggesting, can only be an expression of what Plato thinks human nature is or should be like. Scipio's procedure, in contrast, will be to view human nature as it is actually revealed in a historical society.

The Origin of Society

In keeping with this principle of practicality, the second book of Cicero's *On the Republic* consists in an investigation of the genesis of what he takes to be an actually just society, that of Rome. Only after this investigation does Cicero turn to a consideration of the advantage or disadvantage of justice. This is a further point of contrast between the approaches of Plato and Cicero. In Plato, the question of justice leads to the discussion of the just city. In Cicero, the discussion of a just city leads to the question of justice. Whereas in Plato the initial interest is what justice means for an individual, Cicero is immediately concerned with justice in society as a whole. Towards the end of Book 2, Scipio states the issue in this manner:

> We must consider all the statements we have made so far about the commonwealth as amounting to nothing, and must admit

that we have no basis whatever for further progress, unless we can not merely disprove the contention that a government cannot be carried on without injustice, but are also able to prove positively that it cannot be carried on without the strictest justice.[48]

Scipio maintains that the question of justice cannot be sidestepped, but lies at the root of any political theory. If a commonwealth is necessarily built upon injustice, then this fact must be squarely faced at the beginning of any discussion of politics. If, however, as Scipio maintains, a commonwealth can only be built on justice, then the resulting society will be far different.

This challenge is taken up in *On the Republic* Book 3, where Philus assumes the role that Glaucon played in Plato's *Republic,* stating the case for injustice. Philus criticizes the arguments of Plato and Aristotle by saying that:

> The weakness of their case defeated both their enthusiasm and their eloquence. For the justice which we are investigating is a product of government, not of nature at all; for if it were natural, then like heat and cold, or bitter and sweet, justice and injustice would be the same thing to all men.[49]

Philus proceeds to give examples showing that what is sacred to one society may be abhorrent in another, such as human sacrifice. Surely, he argues, what is natural should be evaluated in the same way in every society. With nature rejected as the basis of justice, it seems

---

[48] *On the Republic* 2.70.

[49] *On the Republic* 3.13.

that there is no source for an absolute standard. Justice would hence be purely conventional.

Furthermore, although justice is praised in the abstract, in reality people only do what is to their own advantage:

> Indeed, men's principles of life are so different that the Cretans and Aetolians consider piracy and brigandage honourable, and the Spartans used to claim as their own all the territory they could touch with their spears. The Athenians also used actually to take public oaths that all lands which produced olives or grain were their own. The Gauls think it disgraceful to grow grain by manual labour; and consequently they go forth armed and reap other men's fields.[50]

Philus's irony is pointed when he refers to the Romans:

> We ourselves, indeed the most just of men, who forbid the races beyond the Alps to plant the olive or the vine, so that our own olive groves and vineyards may be more valuable, are said to act with prudence in doing so, but not with justice; so that you can easily understand that wisdom and equity do not agree.[51]

Popular Roman history extols the virtues of the Roman people, but the reality is far different. It is advantage, rather than virtue, which is the true motivating force.

Philus also notes that not only do ideas of justice vary from place to place, they also change over time, even at Rome. They vary insofar as they are to the advantage of those in power:

---

[50] *On the Republic* 3.15.

[51] *On the Republic* 3.16.

But if I wished to describe the conceptions of justice, and the principles, customs, and habits which have existed, I could show you, not merely differences in all the different nations, but that there have been a thousand changes in a single city, even in our own, in regard to these things. For example, our friend Manilius here, being an interpreter of the law, would give you different advice about the rights of women in regard to legacies and inheritances from that which he used to give in his youth, before the passage of the Voconian law. In fact that law, passed for men's advantage, is full of injustice to women. For why should a woman not have money of her own? Why may a Vestal Virgin have an heir, while her mother may not?[52]

Further, he argues, if justice is really based on nature, how can the standard of justice change within one's lifetime! This consideration leads Philus to affirm Thrasymachus' definition of justice from Plato's *Republic*. Thrasymachus had asserted that justice was simply "the advantage of the stronger."[53] Rather than there being an unchanging content of justice, the idea of justice will vary depending on who or what group is in power:

[If nature][54] had provided laws for us, then all men would obey the same laws, and the same men would not have different laws at different times. But, I ask, if it is the duty of a just and good man to obey the laws, what laws is he to obey? All the different laws that exist? But virtue does not allow inconsistency, nor

---

[52] *On the Republic* 3.17.

[53] *Republic* 1.338c.

[54] The beginning of this passage is missing. Keyes in the Loeb translation supplies "If the supreme God." Rudd inserts "If nature," which is followed here as being more likely in context. *The Republic and The Laws*, trans. Niall Rudd (Oxford: Oxford UP, 1998), 64. See 3.13 quoted above.

does nature permit variation; and laws are imposed on us by fear of punishment, not by our sense of justice. Therefore there is no such thing as natural justice, and from this it follows that neither are men just by nature.[55]

And, Philus queries, if justice were truly founded on nature, should it not also apply to nonhumans as well? He asks, "What is it, if anything, that we are to grant to dumb animals as their due? For it is not men of mediocre talents, but those who are eminent and learned, such as Pythagoras and Empedocles, who declare that the same principles of justice apply to all living creatures, and insist that inevitable penalties threaten those who injure an animal."[56] Is not the limiting of justice to human beings another sign of the arbitrariness of our standards of justice? Philus argues that there is no foundation for granting human beings a special status.

Furthermore, why would one want to be just? Like Thrasymachus, Philus presents justice as, at best, a necessary evil:

> But when there is mutual fear, man fearing man and class fearing class, then, because no one is confident in his strength, a sort of bargain is made between the common people and the powerful; this results in the mixed form of government which Scipio has been recommending; and thus, not nature or desire, but weakness, is the mother of justice.[57]

---

[55] *On the Republic* 3.18.

[56] *On the Republic* 3.19.

[57] *On the Republic* 3.23.

Justice thus is arrived at as a compromise between the greatest advantage and the greatest disadvantage:

> For we must choose one of three things—to do injustice and not to suffer it, or both to do it and to suffer it, or else neither to do it nor suffer it. The happiest choice is to do it with impunity, if you can; the second best is neither to do it nor to suffer it; and the worst fate of all is to engage in the everlasting struggle of doing and suffering injustice."[58]

This claim echoes Glaucon's challenge in Plato's *Republic*: the best life is to take what one wants. The worst is to be taken from. Justice represents a compromise, a second best option. Clearly, Philus states, no one would be just unless under compulsion. The advantages of injustice far outweigh the advantages of acting in a consistently just manner.

In fact, Philus argues, the greatest happiness is found in injustice. This is true not just for individuals, but for societies as well:

> Wisdom urges us to increase our resources, to multiply our wealth, to extend our boundaries; for what is the meaning of those words of praise inscribed on the monuments of our greatest generals, "He extended the boundaries of the empire," except that an addition was made out of the territory of others? Wisdom urges us also to rule over as many subjects as possible, to enjoy pleasures, to become rich, to be rulers and masters; justice, on the other hand, instructs us to spare all men, to consider the interests of the whole human race, to give everyone his due, and not to touch sacred or public property, or that which belongs to others.[59]

---

[58] *On the Republic* 3.23.

[59] *On the Republic* 3.24.

A just society, Philus claims, is a weak society – and one that will probably quickly become an extinct society. Hence, an adequate discussion of justice will need to consider relations between societies as well as between individuals.

It is worth noting that Cicero gives more attention than Plato to the question of international relations. Plato's city will pursue a rather devious foreign policy to allow it to survive when surrounded by larger, more powerful cities. Whether the methods employed, bribing other cities to be allies and stirring up factions in the attacking cities, are just or not is passed over in silence.[60] Plato does later introduce the idea that Greeks should treat other Greeks like fellow citizens, but the idea is based on there being a natural friendship among Greeks rather than strict justice.[61] In any event, this idea remains undeveloped in the *Republic*.

In contrast to the passing comments made in Plato's *Republic*, what sort of obligations we might have to other societies is an important theme in *On the Republic* 3. It is on this theme that we find a memorable anecdote, generally considered to be from Philus's speech. Unfortunately, we have only a fragment of it in the text of the *On the Republic*, which says, "For when he was asked what wickedness drove him to harass the sea with his one pirate galley, he replied, 'The same wickedness that drives you to harass the whole world.'"[62] A fuller version of the story is given by Augustine of Hippo in his *City of God*. It is generally thought that Augustine's source is the missing passage of Cicero:

---

[60] *Republic* 4.422a-423a.

[61] *Republic* 5.471b.

[62] *On the Republic* 3.24. The fragment is found in Nonius (4th-5th century).

Justice being taken away, then, what are kingdoms but great robberies? For what are robberies themselves, but little kingdoms? The band itself is made up of men; it is ruled by the authority of a prince, it is knit together by the pact of the confederacy; the booty is divided by the law agreed on. If, by the admittance of abandoned men, this evil increases to such a degree that it holds places, fixes abodes, takes possession of cities, and subdues peoples, it assumes the more plainly the name of a kingdom, because the reality is now manifestly conferred on it, not by the removal of covetousness, but by the addition of impunity. Indeed, that was an apt and true reply which was given to Alexander the Great by a pirate who had been seized. For when that king had asked the man what he meant by keeping hostile possession of the sea, he answered with bold pride, "What you mean by seizing the whole earth; but because I do it with a petty ship, I am called a robber, whilst you who dost it with a great fleet art styled emperor."[63]

The story of the pirate related by Cicero and Augustine underscores the all-pervasiveness of the question of justice. Whereas Plato focused on the interrelationship of the citizens of his idealized Polis and ignored the question of what is owed to other cities, Cicero wants to bring the latter to the fore. If justice really has a foundation in nature, then it cannot be limited to members of one's own community. In the anecdote, both the pirate captain and Alexander seem to follow the same principle. Alexander can only complain that the pirate is plundering what he himself has already plundered and has the greater power to hold. This corresponds to the understanding of justice held by Thrasymachus, that justice is the "advantage of the

---

[63] Augustine, *The City of God*, trans. Marcus Dodd (New York: The Modern Library, 1950) 112-113, IV.4.

stronger." But the pirate captain shrewdly punctures Alexander's sense of superiority. What separates them, the pirate claims, is not their view of justice, but the force that they possess.

As a conclusion to his speech, Philus restates Glaucon's challenge:

> Let us imagine that...the good man is harassed, attacked, and arrested; blinded, sentenced, bound, branded, banished, and reduced to beggary, and finally is also most justly deemed by all men to be most miserable. Then let the wicked man, on the contrary, be praised, courted, and universally loved; let him receive all sorts of public offices, military commands, wealth and riches from every source; and finally, let him have the universal reputation of being the best man in the world and most worthy of all the favours of fortune. Now I ask you, who could be so insane as to doubt which of the two he would prefer to be?[64]

This brings the discussion back to Philus's initial contention: justice is not intrinsically desirable. Rather, justice is only sought for the benefits one gains from the reputation one has for being just. He broadens his argument to include nations as well as individuals: "the same thing is true of States as of persons; no people would be so foolish as not to prefer to be unjust masters rather than just slaves."[65]

Philus's arguments may be summarized under two headings:

1) Justice is sought only for benefits and to avoid punishment, not for itself.

---

[64] *On the Republic* 3.27.

[65] *On the Republic* 3.28.

2) Justice is not an absolute. Hence it is not natural, but conventional.

Laelius Defends Justice

Laelius is charged with the task of defending justice against Philus's criticisms. Laelius' response is, unfortunately, even less well preserved than Philus's speech. However, the extant text is still sufficient to uncover the general lines of Cicero's treatment of the foundation of justice.[66] The rest of this present work will be in large measure an attempt to reveal how Cicero would answer the questions that arise from his initial exposition of the nature of justice as presented through Laelius.

Laelius's response involves two points that will be developed in greater depth in Cicero's ethical works. His first point constitutes a response to Philus's claim that there is no natural standard for justice. Laelius will counter by referring to a standard of natural law. He begins by giving a surprising definition of law, that "true law is right reason

---

[66] The entire fragment, *On the Republic* 3.33, is preserved in Lactantius' *Divinae Institutiones* VI, 8. 6-9. "True law is right reason in agreement with nature; it is of universal application, unchanging and everlasting; it summons to duty by its commands, and averts from wrongdoing by its prohibitions. And it does not lay its commands or prohibitions on good men in vain, though neither have any effect on the wicked. It is a sin to try to alter this law, nor is it allowable to attempt to repeal any part of it, and it is impossible to abolish it entirely. We cannot be freed from its obligations by senate or people, and we need not look outside ourselves for an expounder or interpreter of it. And there will not be different laws at Rome and at Athens, or different laws now and in the future, but one eternal and unchangeable law will be valid for all nations and all times, and there will be one master and ruler, that is, God, over us all, for he is the author of this law, its promulgator, and its enforcing judge. Whoever is disobedient is fleeing from himself and denying his human nature, and by reason of this very fact he will suffer the worst penalties, even if he escapes what is commonly called punishment."

in agreement with nature."[67] For Thrasymachus, law was simply the will of the ruler. Laelius, in contrast, identifies law fundamentally with reason rather than with will, and reason that is in congruence with the order of nature. He explains further that this law "is of universal application, unchanging and everlasting; it summons to duty by its commands, and averts from wrongdoing by its prohibitions. And it does not lay its commands or prohibitions on good men in vain, though neither have any effect on the wicked."[68]

Furthermore, against Philus's second point, Laelius asserted that this law is unchangeable. For "it is a sin to try to alter this law, nor is it allowable to attempt to repeal any part of it, and it is impossible to abolish it entirely. We cannot be freed from its obligations by senate or people."[69] Finally, Laelius denies that this natural source of justice is unknowable: since "we need not look outside ourselves for an expounder or interpreter of it."[70]

On the face of it, Laelius's claim is rather surprising. He maintains, against Philus, not only that there is an absolute standard, a universal natural law, but that it is seemingly one of the most knowable things. Where does this law come from? About this law, Laelius says, "there will be one master and ruler, that is, God, over us all, for he is the author of this law, its promulgator, and its enforcing judge." How does God as the author of natural law relate to his earlier contention that law represents "right reason in agreement with nature?" Does this

---

[67] *On the Republic* 3.33.

[68] *On the Republic* 3.33.

[69] *On the Republic* 3.33.

[70] *On the Republic* 3.33.

dependence presuppose a theology that Laelius has not explained or defended? What is the content of this law, and how would one know what it is? Laelius does not here explain.

Even if one were to agree with Laelius that there is a discoverable natural law, the question might be asked: Why should I follow this law? Or, to put in another way, why give up my own advantage to follow the commands of the natural law? In reply to this question, Laelius offers the paradox that "whoever is disobedient is fleeing from himself and denying his human nature, and by reason of this very fact he will suffer the worst penalties, even if he escapes what is commonly called punishment."[71] Somehow the worst punishment is disobeying the law in and of itself. Why is this so? Laelius suggests that what Philus claims is our advantage is really not.

Laelius's claims may be summarized in two points:

1) There is a universal, unchanging natural law which is the basis for justice.
2) Acting in accordance with this law is intrinsically advantageous.

This leads to two major questions to be explored in coming to understand Cicero's ethical theory:

1) What is the natural law, how is it known, and what is its content?
2) What is the reason to follow it?

---

[71] *On the Republic* 3.33.

The first question will be examined in the next chapters (3 and 4). The second question will be the focus of chapter 5.

Summary

We have examined the exchange between Philus and Laelius as a means to see how Cicero approaches the question of justice. In Philus's comments we encounter some of the chief objections to the very intelligibility of justice, as well as a critique of what is commonly meant by the term. Laelius offers an intriguing, if underdeveloped defence of the reality of justice and its value. The purpose of this present chapter has been to provide an initial orientation to the question rather than to provide a definite Ciceronian answer.

CHAPTER III
The Foundation and Meaning of Natural Law

Cicero's fullest treatment of natural law is to be found in his dialogue *On the Laws*.[72] This dialogue features Cicero himself and two of his closest friends as the speakers. These are his brother, Quintus, and Atticus, an adherent of the Epicurean philosophy.[73] As with his *On the Republic*, Cicero takes his inspiration from a work of Plato. In this case, the work is Plato's dialogue the *Laws*. The two works have many similarities, but they also differ in significant ways. A striking difference

---

[72] The surviving text of *Laws* is not complete. *Laws* originally consisted of at least five books. Fortunately for the present purpose, however, the primary loss of text is in the absence of the final books. Cicero's treatment of natural law is to be found in the first book and the beginning of the second. The surviving manuscripts contain books 1, 2, and most of book 3. For discussions of the textual situation, see James E. G. Zetzel, introduction to *On the Commonwealth and On the Laws*, Cambridge Texts in the History of Philosophy (Cambridge: Cambridge UP, 1999), xx-xxii and Andrew R. Dyck, *A Commentary on Cicero, De Legibus* (Ann Arbor: U of Michigan Press, 2004), 28-30, 40-45.

[73] For further information on the setting and characters of *Laws*, see Powell's introduction in: *The Republic and The Laws*, trans. Niall Rudd (Oxford: Oxford UP, 1998), xviii-xx.

between Plato's and Cicero's treatments is what happens in the first book of both works. Plato's *Laws* has, at least on the surface, a very limited purpose, the developing of a practical law code for a new city to be founded in Crete. In contrast, Cicero begins his *On the Laws* with a discussion of the theoretical underpinnings for good laws before giving a law code in the later books. Hence, Cicero will have to discuss anthropological and metaphysical issues before the nominal theme of the work, human law, is considered:

> You must understand that in no other kind of discussion can one bring out so clearly what Nature's gifts to man are, what a wealth of most excellent possessions the human mind enjoys, what the purpose is, to strive after and accomplish which we have been born and placed in this world, what it is that unites men, and what natural fellowship there is among them. *For it is only after all these things have been made clear that the origin of Law and Justice can be discovered.* [emphasis added][74]

These philosophical issues, namely those regarding human nature, are not the sort of background generally expected, in Cicero's time or our own, as a prelude to a discussion of laws. Atticus expresses his surprise, and asks, "Then do you not think that the science of law is to be derived from the praetor's edict, as the majority do now, or from the Twelve Tables, as people used to think, but from the deepest mysteries of philosophy?[75]

Atticus correctly concludes that Cicero will be arguing against the idea that law is grounded merely on positive legislation or custom.

---

[74] *On the Laws* 1.16.

[75] *On the Laws* 1.17.

Hence his treatment of laws is not intended, primarily, as a handbook for lawyers, but is meant to uncover the foundation of law itself. He explains that "in our present investigation we intend to cover the whole range of universal Justice and Law in such a way that our own civil law, as it is called, will be confined to a small and narrow corner. For we must explain the nature of Justice, and this must be sought for in the nature of man.[76] The phrase "the nature of Justice...must be sought for in the nature of man" could function as a summary of the contents of the first book of *On the Laws*.

Cicero will not consider only personal moral conduct, but also "...the laws by which States ought to be governed."[77] From this will follow a consideration of "the enactments and decrees of nations which are already formulated and put in writing."[78] A consideration of the legal ramifications of natural law is what, in the judgement of classical scholar Marcia L. Colish, distinguishes Cicero from his predecessors:

> Cicero develops the Stoic doctrine of natural law well beyond the point to which the Stoics themselves had taken it. He translates the Stoic idea of natural law as an ethical and cosmic principle into a legal principle to be used as the norm of the legitimacy of the civil law of a given historical community. This is an important and creative accomplishment and one destined to be extremely influential in post-classical legal and political thought.[79]

---

[76] *On the Laws* 1.17.

[77] *On the Laws* 1.17.

[78] *On the Laws* 1.17.

[79] Marcia L. Colish, *The Stoic Tradition from Antiquity to the Early Middle Ages: I. Stoicism in Classical Latin Literature* (Leiden: Brill, 1985), 96.

Those looking for originality in Cicero, Colish indicates, may find it in his application of natural law to civil law. Or, to use academic classifications, for the Stoics natural law was chiefly a topic in ethics and metaphysics. For Cicero natural law is ultimately a topic, perhaps *the* topic, in political philosophy. Rather than being themselves the highest arbiter, as Philus suggested, the laws of a nation are themselves to be evaluated in reference to an independent standard.

The Meaning of Natural Law

Cicero's definition of law is perhaps more accurately described as a series of interrelated definitions of law. His first articulation is that "Law is the highest reason, implanted in Nature, which commands what ought to be done and forbids the opposite. This reason, when firmly fixed and fully developed in the human mind, is Law."[80] This first formulation has two elements. Cicero first connects law with the rational order of nature. He thus harks back to earlier philosophers: directly to the Stoics, but ultimately to a Platonic and Aristotelian idea of the orderly nature of the universe.[81] Right conduct means acting in accordance with the rational order. Secondly, when human reason is in agreement with the highest reason it is law. One is reminded of Kant's conception of the autonomous person being both subject to the law, but also a legislator insofar as he acts according to reason.[82] Unlike

---

[80] *On the Laws* 1.18-19.

[81] Particularly seen in Plato's *Timaeus* and in book 12 of Aristotle's *Metaphysics*. Cicero gives an extensive quotation on this theme from Aristotle's lost dialogue *On Philosophy* in his *The Nature of the Gods* 2.95.

[82] See for example, Kant's *Grounding for the Metaphysics of Morals*, Second Section, paragraph 432.

Kant, however, Cicero will not attempt to derive his moral precepts from pure reason without considering human nature.[83]

Cicero further states that "now if this is correct, as I think it to be in general, then the origin of Justice is to be found in Law, for Law is a natural force; it is the mind and reason of the intelligent man, the standard by which Justice and Injustice are measured."[84] To connect this thought back to the understanding of justice as giving what is due, one might say that what is due is what is in accordance with nature. And this can be discovered by human reason. Furthermore, Cicero asserts, "in determining what Justice is, let us begin with that supreme Law which had its origin ages before any written law existed or any State had been established."[85] Even the laws of states are to be referred back to a natural law. There is a possible appeal beyond the laws of one's own society. Hence Cicero claims a human law derives its authority from the nature of things:

> But we must come to the true understanding of the matter, which is as follows: this and other commands and prohibitions of nations have the power to summon to righteousness and away from wrong-doing; but this power is not merely older than the existence of nations and States, it is coeval with that God who guards and rules heaven and earth.[86]

---

[83] Kant's view of the moral law will be compared to that of Cicero in chapter 4.

[84] *On the Laws* 1.19.

[85] *On the Laws* 1.19.

[86] *On the Laws* 2.10.

Hence natural law has always existed, being coexistent with God. Furthermore, the natural law does not function only as a prohibition "away from wrongdoing," but also provides a positive goal by having "the power to summon to righteousness." Natural law is not merely a list of prohibitions, but will reveal a good to be pursued.

As should be readily apparent, Cicero's position rests on several important presuppositions about the nature of reality and human nature. Cicero himself is aware of this dependence. In the remainder of the first book of *On the Laws* he explains three presuppositions that he argues are required for the acceptance of a natural law.

The First Presupposition of Natural Law: Nature is Ruled by the Gods

The first presupposition is "that it is by the might of the immortal gods, or by their nature, reason, power, mind, will, or any other term which may make my meaning clearer, that all Nature is governed."[87] This first presupposition may be viewed as actually comprising two claims. Firstly, divine beings exist and they govern nature in some fashion. In Cicero's explanation of natural law this first presupposition addresses a fundamental question that can be asked of any law: who is the lawmaker? The second element in this first presupposition is that the governing or ruling of nature is rational. Cicero rules out the capricious gods associated with popular mythology. Rather, the gods display the highest reason in their governing of the universe.

Cicero recognizes that without receiving acceptance of this premise, he cannot proceed: "For if you do not admit it, we must begin our

---

[87] *On the Laws* 1.21.

argument with this problem before taking up anything else."[88] Perhaps disappointingly, Atticus is willing to grant this premise for the sake of continuing the discussion. He meekly comments that "surely I will grant it, if you insist upon it, for the singing of the birds about us and the babbling of the streams relieve me from all the fear that I may be overheard by any of my comrades in the school."[89] Atticus, as an Epicurean, should have serious objections to Cicero's claim that the gods have a governing role in relationship to the universe. Contrary to popular perception, Epicureans were not officially atheists.[90] However, the Epicureans did deny that the gods paid any attention to human beings. If they did so, their happiness would be lessened due to the care required to oversee human affairs. Atticus' willingness to not argue this point simplifies the dialogue tremendously (or perhaps makes the dialogue possible) but also relieves Cicero of the need to prove this premise.

What would Cicero have said if Atticus had objected? More than a decade would elapse before Cicero would write a dialogue on this theme, *On the Nature of the Gods*. In the introduction to that work, he explains the difficulty of his subject matter:

> There are a number of branches of philosophy that have not as yet been by any means adequately explored; but the inquiry

---

[88] *On the Laws* 1.21.

[89] *On the Laws* 1.21.

[90] Though they were often thought to be so in secret, according to Cotta in Cicero's *On the Nature of the Gods* 1.123. For Epicurus' affirmation of the existence of the gods and our knowledge of them, see his *Letter to Menoeceus* in Diogenes Laertius' *Lives of Eminent Philosophers* 10.123-124. For a fuller discussion of Epicurus and the gods, see John Rist, *Epicurus: An Introduction* (New York: Cambridge UP, 1972), 140-63.

into the nature of the gods, which is both highly interesting in relation to the theory of the soul, and fundamentally important for the regulation of religion, is one of special difficulty and obscurity.[91]

Cicero is quite candid in recognizing that resolving philosophically whether or not the gods exist and their nature are not issues to be easily or swiftly resolved. His *On the Nature of the Gods* eschews an easy philosophical resolution. Cicero's dodge at this point in the *On the Laws* may be viewed as an indication of his good sense. An adequate response to Atticus could itself be a long dialogue or series of dialogues.

The exact nature of the gods is also left open to interpretation. His characterization "that it is by the might of the immortal gods, or by their nature, reason, power, mind, will, or any other term which may make my meaning clearer, that all Nature is governed,"[92] seems to have been drawn up with a view to being acceptable to Platonists, Peripatetics, and Stoics, as well as religious believers. What is required, Cicero indicates, is not a creator God or gods, but (a) being(s) who *rationally* govern the universe. Cicero puts many arguments for this position in the mouth of the Stoic Balbus in *On the Nature of the Gods*.[93] How seriously one takes these to be arguments that Cicero himself would agree with seems largely to depend on whether Cicero's theological utterances are considered to be sincere, or merely as

---

[91] *On the Nature of the Gods* 1.1.

[92] *On the Laws* 1.21.

[93] See especially *On the Nature of the Gods* 2.1-44, 73-168.

propaganda for the non-philosophical.[94] This lack of a developed theological justification is disappointing for those hoping for a more exhaustive and thoroughgoing demonstration of the foundations of natural law from first principles, but such a justification or demonstration must be looked for else-where. [95]

It is interesting to note the shifting back and forth Cicero does between *gods* and *God*. His polytheistic utterances might seem to be at odds with his other references to a God, such as when he argues for the divine mind as the source of law:

> For the divine mind cannot exist without reason, and divine reason cannot but have this power to establish right and wrong... For reason did exist, derived from the Nature of the universe, urging men to right conduct and diverting them from wrongdoing, and this reason did not first become Law when it was written down, but when it first came into existence; and it came into existence simultaneously with the divine mind.[96]

What is the nature of this divine mind? Here the divine being he is describing sounds like a transcendent and all wise God one associates

---

[94] For an example of the latter position, see Arthur Stanley Pease, "The Conclusion of Cicero's *the Nature of the Gods*," *Transactions and Proceedings of the American Philological Association* 44 (1913): 25-37. For recent reappraisals, see David Fott, "The Politico-Philosophical Character of Cicero's Verdict in *De Natura Deorum*," in *Cicero's Practical Philosophy*, ed. Walter Nicgorski (South Bend, Ind: University of Notre Dame Press, 2012), 152-180, and J. P. F. Wynne, *Cicero on the Philosophy of Religion: On the Nature of the Gods and On Divination* (New York: Cambridge UP, 2019).

[95] For an attempt to construct a Ciceronian theology from his works, see Martin van den Bruwaene, *La Théologie de Cicéron* (Louvain: Bibliothèque de l'Université, 1937).

[96] *On the Laws* 2.10.

with monotheistic religions, not Roman polytheism. Yet his very next statement is that "the true and primal Law, applied to command and prohibition, is the right reason of supreme Jupiter."[97]

One may see in this an attempt to harmonize the popular polytheism of his time with what one might call philosophical monotheism. This tension goes back at least to Plato.[98] In his dialogue the *Timaeus*, the titular character speaks of a "father of this universe" in distinction from the gods.[99] Aristotle in his *Metaphysics* discusses both the Unmoved Mover and also the many lesser movers of the spheres.[100] Aristotle also attempts, somewhat ambivalently, to connect the celestial movers to the gods of mythology.[101] One might also see in Cicero the influence of the Stoic idea that the gods are merely representations or manifestations of the one God.[102] Although Cicero grants that there may be many divine rational beings, the unity of the universe is due to an ultimate mind. Hence, in the second book of *On the Laws* he goes so far as to call this ultimate being of the philosophers Jupiter.[103]

---

[97] *On the Laws* 2.10.

[98] The Presocratic philosopher Xenophanes held that the popular conception of the gods was deficient. However, he, apparently, made no attempt to harmonize his view with Greek mythology. See Patricia Curd, ed., *A Presocratics Reader: Selected Fragments and Testimonia*, trans. Richard D. McKirahan (Indianapolis: Hackett, 1996), 25-28.

[99] *Timaeus* 28e. See also Timaeus' comparison of the gods as the celestial bodies versus the mythological gods at 40d-41a.

[100] *Metaphysics* 12.8.

[101] *Metaphysics* 12.8 1074b1-15.

[102] *The Nature of the Gods* 2.70-71. This is the view of Zeno of Citium, the founder of Stoicism, see Diogenes Laertius 7.147.

[103] *On the Laws* 2.10.

The Second Presupposition of Natural Law: Human Beings Share in Reason

Cicero's second presupposition is that human beings have a special status due to being rational. He explains "that animal which we call man, endowed with foresight and quick intelligence, complex, keen, possessing memory, full of reason and prudence, has been given a certain distinguished status by the supreme God who created him."[104] Our special status is seen in how human life differs from the life of other living beings. It is reason that allows human beings to live beyond the immediate physical concerns that characterize non-rational animals. Cicero identifies the essence of reasoning to be not in solving problems immediately to hand, but in looking further afield through rising from sense knowledge to an understanding of the causes of things and the long-range consequences of our actions. He elaborates this point in his dialogue *On Ends*:

> Nature has bestowed on man the gift of reason, of an active, vigorous intelligence, able to carry on several operations at the same time with extreme speed, and having, so to speak, a keen scent to discern the causes and effects of things, to draw analogies, combine things separate, connect the future with the present, and survey the entire field of the subsequent course of life.[105]

Because of these consequences of being rational, human society is characterized by a complex web of social interactions. These complex

---

[104] *On the Laws* 1.22.

[105] *On Ends* 2.45.

interactions are made possible in large measure by the power of speech, which Cicero calls "the most effective promoter of human intercourse."[106]

Furthermore, Cicero holds not only that reason makes complex social relations possible, but in fact that rational beings are essentially social. Recall again the statement of Xenocrates to which Cicero gave his approval at the beginning of *On the Republic*. When asked what advantage is to be obtained from his teaching, he responds that his disciples learned "to do of their own accord what they are compelled to do by the law."[107] Xenocrates, and Cicero, are saying that to be more fully rational is to be more fully a well-integrated member of a community. This is not just a case of an enlightened self-interest, but the natural outflow of a rational nature. Cicero affirms that "as swarms of bees do not gather for the sake of making honeycomb but make the honeycomb because they are gregarious by nature, so human beings—and to a much higher degree—exercise their skill together in action and thought because they are naturally gregarious."[108]

Cicero's point is that bees do not deliberate as to whether or not to join with their fellow bees in making a honeycomb and then, based on that calculation, decide to participate. Rather, it is the bee's nature to be a social being. This social nature manifests itself in the activity of honeycomb making. Cicero considers this to be true of human beings as well. To return to *On Ends*:

> It is reason moreover that has inspired man with a relish for his kind; she has produced a natural conformity both of language

---

[106] *On the Laws* 1.27.

[107] *On the Republic* 1.3.

[108] *On Duties* 1.157.

and habit; she has prompted the individual, starting from friendship and from family affection, to expand his interests, forming social ties first with his fellow-citizens and later with all mankind.[109]

Once again it is worth noting the broad view that Cicero is taking. He does not view natural human relations as restricted to family, friends, and fellow citizens, but looks to "all mankind" as forming a community.

But if being social is a consequence of being rational, what principle is to govern human relations? This question is addressed by Cicero's third presupposition.

Third Presupposition: Human Nature is to Share in Justice

The third presupposition Cicero discusses is that "we have been made by nature to share justice amongst ourselves and to impart it to one another."[110] Following from the second presupposition, Cicero is arguing that sharing in reason imposes obligations. This third proposition is derived from our human nature to be a social being. Reason, he had claimed, makes us naturally social beings. But without justice life in society is not possible.[111]

Furthermore, reason makes individuals not just part of a human community. Recall that his first presupposition rested on the assumption

---

[109] *On Ends* 2.45.

[110] *On the Laws* 1.33. Rudd's translation, based on recent scholarship. For a discussion of the textual issues and problems of interpretation for this passage, see Dyck, *De Legibus* 155-156.

[111] In *On the Republic* 1.39 Cicero had Scipio state that a commonwealth required people "associated in an agreement with respect to justice and a partnership for the common good."

that the gods are rational. This sharing in reason is a uniting factor between the gods and human beings: "Therefore, since there is nothing better than reason, and since it exists in both man and God, the first common possession of man and God is reason."[112] The possession of reason reveals a common element between beings that might otherwise seem to have nothing in common. Furthermore, he adds that "those who have reason in common must also have right reason in common. And since right reason is Law, we must believe that men have Law also in common with the gods."[113] If law is conformity with reason, beings that share in reason, in some fashion share the same law. And sharing in law, Cicero holds, means being members of a community:

> Further, those who share Law must also share Justice; and those who share these are to be regarded as members of one commonwealth. If indeed they obey the same authorities and powers, this is true in a far greater degree; but as a matter of fact they do obey this celestial system, the divine mind, and the God of transcendent power. Hence we must now conceive of this whole universe as one commonwealth of which both gods and men are members.[114]

Here Cicero appeals to the principle that being under common laws means sharing in justice. Cicero takes an initially political principle, justice, and gives it a cosmological significance. Human beings and the gods share in reason and hence have justice in common.

---

[112] *On the Laws* 1.23.

[113] *On the Laws* 1.23.

[114] *On the Laws* 1.23.

In fact, God (precise nature undetermined) is the ultimate origin of the law that is the standard for determining what is just.

One might consider as a fourth presupposition, not made explicit by Cicero, the principle that:

> Human reason is able to be in conformity with reason itself. This makes human knowledge of the natural law possible.

It is worth noting that Cicero himself does not seem to consider the resolution of the question of the nature of the highest good essential to his presentation of natural law. In *On the Laws* he considers various views about the nature of the highest good.[115] Cicero ultimately concludes that a precise resolution as to the nature of the highest good is unnecessary for their discussion.[116]

The Epistemological Status of the Presuppositions

Surprisingly, it is from the mouth of Atticus that Cicero provides a summary of his three presuppositions:

> How can I help being convinced, when it has just been proved to us, first, that we have been provided and equipped with what we may call the gifts of the gods; next, that there is only one principle by which men may live with one another, and that this is the same for all, and possessed equally by all; and finally, that all men are bound together by a certain natural feeling of kindliness and goodwill, and also by a partnership in Justice? Now that we have

---

[115] *On the Laws* 1.52-57.

[116] *On the Laws* 1.57.

admitted the truth of these conclusions, and rightly, I think, how can we separate Law and Justice from Nature?[117]

A very shocking admission for an Epicurean to make!

What status does Cicero think these presuppositions have? Shortly after Atticus' summary Cicero admits that "I cannot expect that they will be universally accepted, for this is impossible."[118] He is, perhaps, merely being realistic by not expecting universal assent. Cicero himself was well aware of the unending disputes between the various philosophical schools, a phenomenon that is still with us today. One of his most quoted passages is that "somehow or other no statement is too absurd for some philosophers to make."[119] This does not mean that Cicero does not believe these propositions to be true. He simply admits that they are not susceptible of mathematical-style proof. However, he does expect "the approval of all who believe that everything which is right and honourable is to be desired for its own sake, and that nothing whatever is to be accounted a good unless it is praiseworthy in itself, or at least nothing should be considered a great good unless it can rightly be praised for its own sake."[120]

Cicero's key point is that not all goods are means to an end; rather, some goods are truly sought for their own sake. In particular, the goods that are sought for their own sake are the right and honorable. The honorable (honestum) will be a key concept in understanding Cicero's ethical philosophy. He will define this in his *On Ends* as "that which is

---

[117] *On the Laws* 1.35.

[118] *On the Laws* 1.37.

[119] *On Divination* 2.119.

[120] *On the Laws* 1.37.

of such a nature that, though devoid of all utility, it can justly be commended in and for itself, apart from any profit or reward."[121] This understanding of the honorable pinpoints a fundamental disagreement between Cicero and the position, suggested by Glaucon (in Plato's *Republic*) and Philus (in *On the Republic*), that only satisfying one's appetites is a good sought for its own sake and justice and other supposed virtues are merely means to that end. Cicero is thus indicating that what is required to accept the principles of natural law is the agreement that certain goods, the right and honorable, are intrinsically desirable.

Cicero does think that there can be found a broad consensus on his principles by people of virtue. Among such people he would include followers of what he regards as the best philosophical traditions of his day: Platonists, Peripatetics, and Stoics. The dissenting voices are those of the Epicureans and the Skeptics. The Epicurean desire for an undisturbed and private life he considers to be in contradiction to the requirements of life in society. Hence, he has to remind Atticus of his willingness to bracket his Epicurean objections or else they will have to drop the current discussion:

> So far, however, as those philosophers are concerned who practise self-indulgence, are slaves to their own bodies, and test the desirability of everything on the basis of pleasure and pain, let us, even if they are right (for there is no need to quarrel with them here), bid them carry on their discussions in their own gardens,[122] and even request them to abstain for a while from

---

[121] *On Ends* 2.45.

[122] Epicurus and his disciples gathered in his garden.

taking part in matters affecting the State, which they neither understand nor have ever wished to understand.[123]

The Academic Skeptic position, which Cicero adopted as his approach, is also problematical. Hence, he continues:

> And let us implore the Academy—the new one, formed by Arcesilaus and Carneades—to be silent, since it contributes nothing but confusions to all these problems; for if it should attack what we think we have constructed and arranged so beautifully, it would play too great havoc with it; at the same time I should like to win over this school, and so do not dare to banish it from the discussion.[124]

Cicero seems to be expressing the hope that he can persuade skeptics to at least give him a docile hearing. This perhaps harkens back to his goal of attaining the greatest probability rather than absolute certitude.[125] He thinks that his account will seem most in accord with our experience of human reality, particularly that of humans as social beings.

---

[123] *On the Laws* 1.39.

[124] *On the Laws* 1.39. There is a lacuna in the text after this sentence.

[125] Much has been written on the interpretation of this passage. See J. P. Glucker, "Cicero's Philosophical Affiliations," *The Question of "Eclecticism"*, ed. J. Dillon and A. A. Long (Berkeley: U of California P, 1988), 34-69; W. Görler, "Silencing the Troublemaker: *De Legibus* I.39 and the Continuity of Cicero's Skepticism," *Cicero the Philosopher: Twelve Papers*, ed. J. G. F. Powell (Oxford: Oxford UP, 1995), 85-113.

Summary

In the third book of *On the Republic* and in the first and beginning of the second books of *On the Laws*, Cicero has presented a coherent, plausible account of the grounding of natural law.

He stated that there are three assumptions that are prerequisite for the existence of natural law:

1) Nature is rationally ordered/ruled by a divine mind
2) Human beings share in Reason, i.e., are rational
3) From being rational, it follows that we are social beings, and hence share in justice

To this one might add a further Ciceronian principle that:

Human reason is able to be in conformity with reason itself. This makes human knowledge of the natural law possible.

These principles represent Cicero's essential position on the nature of the natural law. In order to clarify more fully his vision, it may be useful to compare Cicero's approach to natural law with later, better-known versions. Due to their influence and familiarity, perhaps the most helpful for consideration are the positions of Thomas Aquinas and Immanuel Kant. This will be the topic of the next chapter.

CHAPTER IV
Moral Law in Cicero,
Aquinas, and Kant

To illuminate Cicero's account of natural law, it may be useful at this stage to compare his treatment with later influential accounts of moral law. Due to their influence and familiarity, perhaps the most helpful for consideration are the positions of Thomas Aquinas (1225-1274) and Immanuel Kant (1724-1804).

Cicero and Aquinas on Law[126]

Let us first consider the natural law as presented by Aquinas. He develops his treatment within the framework of examining law in general.[127] Aquinas defines law as "an ordinance of reason for the common good, made by him who has care of the community, and

---

[126] For a fuller comparison between Cicero and Aquinas, see Charles Nemeth, *A Comparative Analysis of Cicero and Aquinas: Nature and the Natural Law* (New York: Bloomsbury, 2017).

[127] Aquinas's treatment of law is found in the *Summa Theologiae* I-II Q. 90-108. Natural Law is discussed in question 94.

promulgated."[128] This definition has four components, each of which he considers necessary for a putative law truly to be a law. First, a law must be based on reason. Human acts are (or should be) governed and evaluated by reason. A decree lacking in reasonableness Aquinas considers as being intrinsically defective. He thus will not grant it the status of a law.[129] Even a cursory reading of Cicero's *On the Laws*, as has been shown in the preceding chapter, will reveal that Cicero's attitude seems to express general agreement with this sentiment. This point is made most explicitly when he gives his approval to the definition that "law is the highest reason, implanted in Nature, which commands what ought to be done and forbids the opposite. This reason, when firmly fixed and fully developed in the human mind, is Law."[130] Thus for both Cicero and Aquinas, no reason means no law.

Aquinas's second component is that the purpose of a law is for the common good. He argues that "since every part is ordained to the whole, as imperfect to perfect; and since one man is a part of the perfect community, the law must need regard properly the relationship to universal happiness."[131] Again, this element of his definition seems reasonably straightforward. A law should be for the benefit of the community for which it is intended. It seems that Cicero would strongly agree with this component. As was shown in the last chapter, his *On the Republic* is particularly directed against the idea (represented

---

[128] *Summa Theologiae* I-II, Q. 90, A. 4. Translation is Fathers of the English Dominican Province, 1920 edition, as found online at http://newadvent.org/summa/ (accessed June 7. 2021).

[129] *Summa Theologiae* I-II, Q. 90, A. 1.

[130] *On the Laws* 1.18-19.

[131] *Summa Theologiae* I-II, Q. 90, A. 2.

by Thrasymachus and Philus) that justice could be for the advantage of the ruler without being for the advantage of the community as a whole. Since he states that "the origin of justice is to be found in Law,"[132] one may legitimately infer that law as well ought to be for the common good.

Next, since "to order anything to the common good, belongs either to the whole people, or to someone who is the viceregent of the whole people,"[133] the third part of Aquinas's definition of law is that it must be made by someone who has some kind of care for or authority over the community in question. This component also appears, in the abstract, to be non-controversial. A person lacking in political authority would not be in a position to legislate anything for a community. The real controversy would be who legitimately has the authority for the common good.

Fourthly and finally, a law must be promulgated, that is those to whom it applies must be somehow informed of it. If a law is to achieve the purpose of promoting the common good it must somehow be made known. Cicero appears tacitly to affirm this principle in his own procedure of promulgating his idealized law code in the second and third books of *On the Laws*.

In conclusion, it appears that Cicero would not object to Thomas Aquinas's definition of law. Although he does not explicitly formulate the same definition, it does appear to be conformable with his treatment of law in *On the Laws*. One can then inquire into how

---

[132] *On the Laws* 1.19.

[133] *Summa Theologiae* I-II, Q. 90, A. 3.

Cicero's natural law teaching is relatable to Aquinas's version of natural law when viewed as an application of his definition.

Law and Natural Law

Let us then return to the definition to see how Aquinas applies it to the natural law. To summarize, Aquinas's full definition of law was as "an ordinance of reason for the common good, made by him who has care of the community, and promulgated."[134] In the case of natural law, the reason would be the divine reason.[135] God would also be the one who has care of the universe and is responsible for the common good.

One sees at this stage that a crucial difference between Aquinas's and Cicero's account is in the role of God. In Aquinas God is responsible for creating the universe and is responsible for the natures of the things in it. Thus, he argues that "it is evident, granted that the world is ruled by Divine Providence...that the whole community of the universe is governed by Divine Reason. Wherefore the very Idea of the government of things in God the Ruler of the universe, has the nature of a law."[136] In Aquinas's thought, God is not only a mover of the universe, but exercises a providential oversight.

In contrast, as was considered in Chapter 3, Cicero is ambiguous regarding the divine nature and its relationship to the universe. One could see in Cicero's discussion a transcendent creator God as found in Plato's *Timaeus.* However, one could also interpret his treatment as suggesting a Stoic, pantheistic view of God as simply part of the

---

[134] *Summa Theologiae* I-II, Q. 90, A. 4.

[135] *Summa Theologiae* I-II, Q. 91, A. 2.

[136] *Summa Theologiae* I-II, Q. 91, A. 1.

universe rather than as being distinct from it. As was pointed out above, for Cicero, the exact nature of God is not essential for understanding the natural law. His ethical position is based fundamentally on an understanding of human nature, not on metaphysical speculation. He is candid that his position is not capable of demonstrative proof. But he is equally forceful in his claim that it is the most plausible account of human life and action. That is to say, rival accounts are simply implausible in describing human reality.[137] He considers human nature to be adequately known for his purpose. The good life is a life lived in accordance with our social and rational nature. Natural law thus provides the most plausible background. Natural law does not ground ethics; ethics gives reason to believe in the existence of the natural law.

Perhaps the contrast could be best expressed by saying that Aquinas' approach is top down while Cicero's is bottom up. Aquinas, based on previous arguments in the *Summa*, will begin from the standpoint of a personal God who creates and rules the universe. Cicero, in contrast, takes as his starting point in *On the Laws* human nature and moral experience. For him, human nature grounds one's metaphysical viewpoint.

Hence Holton's criticism that Cicero's position "rests in part on an understanding of divine providence and an anthropocentric teleology which he himself had examined and rejected in two other works,"[138] is based on a misunderstanding of Cicero's project. Cicero is not assuming providence in the Christian sense of the term. A

---

[137] *On Duties* 3.33.

[138] Holton, 171.

pantheistic, immanent theology would work sufficiently for his purpose. Nor do ethics for Cicero depend upon theology.

Cicero and the Intelligibility of Ethics

Cicero's position regarding the intelligibility of ethics might be thought to resemble that of Immanuel Kant. Based on his epistemological principles, Kant argued that God's existence could not be known through speculative philosophy.[139] However, if one accepted the intelligibility of ethics, he thought that one must also accept the truth of certain propositions. These were the existence of God, the immortality of the soul, and freedom.[140] Without these assumptions, Kant thought, ethics would not be possible. So, Kant, like Cicero in *On the Laws*, moves from ethics to metaphysics, rather than conversely.

Although there is a similar movement, it does not seem that the connection should not be pressed too far. Kant's epistemological outlook and structure are foreign to Cicero's approach. Kant is very much focused on seeking certitude and its limits. Cicero, in contrast, is quite satisfied to discover what is probable. For Kant, knowledge seems to be all or nothing: if one does not fully accept ethics, the three presuppositions become meaningless. For Cicero, the demand is less strenuous; good probability is sufficient.

A better recent parallel to Cicero's position might be that found in Thomas Nagel's 2012 book *Mind and Cosmos: Why the Materialist Neo-Darwinian Conception of Nature is Almost Certainly False*. Therein

---

[139] See especially Kant's *Prolegomena to Any Future Metaphysics* Part 3, and more fully in his *Critique of Pure Reason* I.II.II.III: "The Ideal of Pure Reason."

[140] Kant, *Critique of Pure Reason* II.II.2: "The Ideal of the Highest Good, as a Determining Ground of the Ultimate End of Pure Reason."

Nagel argues that any intelligible account of reality must include an adequate account of our moral experience. He claims that "value judgments and moral reasoning are part of human life, and therefore part of the factual evidence about what humans are capable of."[141] Cicero, it seems, would agree. To dismiss ethics as illusionary would be to ignore the evidence. For Cicero, the question then is how one may best account for the reality of ethics. This is to be found in the acceptance of a natural law.

Knowledge of the Natural Law

How does one know the content of the natural law? This question raises the issue, as Thomas Aquinas describes it, of promulgation. By promulgation in the case of the natural law, Aquinas does not mean any kind of supernatural revelation. Rather, he considers it to be promulgated by being our nature. Knowledge of our nature is accessible to investigation and understanding as we scrutinize our "respective inclinations to their proper acts and ends."[142] His point is that natural law is not so much an extrinsic rule imposed upon us, but rather is inseparable from our own nature.[143]

In order to concretize this principle, Aquinas appeals to our human nature as revealed by our natural inclinations. He observes that since humans engage in several levels of activities, our wellbeing is to

---

[141] Thomas Nagel, *Mind and Cosmos: Why the Materialist Neo-Darwinian Conception of Nature is Almost Certainly False* (New York: Oxford UP, 2012), 106.

[142] *Summa Theologiae* I-II, Q. 91, A. 2.

[143] This position is the guiding theme in Jean Porter, *Nature as Reason: A Thomistic Theory of the Natural Law* (Grand Rapids, MI: William B. Eerdmans, 2005).

be found in a hierarchy of good activities.[144] Our most basic good is maintaining our own existence and avoiding harm.[145] However, we also have goods in common with other animals, such as having children and nurturing them.[146] But we are also rational beings, and so:

> Thirdly, there is in man an inclination to good, according to the nature of his reason, which nature is proper to him: thus man has a natural inclination to know the truth about God, and to live in society: and in this respect, whatever pertains to this inclination belongs to the natural law; for instance, to shun ignorance, to avoid offending those among whom one has to live, and other such things regarding the above inclination."[147]

Aquinas thus considers both the speculative and practical applications of reason. On the one hand, to be rational is to be a knower, especially of the causes of things. He thus considers the highest cause, God. Secondly, to be rational is to be social, so he considers the highest social aspect, life in community.

---

[144] *Summa Theologiae* I-II, Q. 94, A. 2. "Wherefore according to the order of natural inclinations, is the order of the precepts of the natural law."

[145] *Summa Theologiae* I-II, Q. 94, A. 2. "There is first of all an inclination to good in accordance with the nature which he has in common with all substances: inasmuch as every substance seeks the preservation of its own being, according to its nature: and by reason of this inclination, whatever is a means of preserving human life, and of warding off its obstacles, belongs to the natural law."

[146] *Summa Theologiae* I-II, Q. 94, A. 2. "Secondly, there is in man an inclination to things that pertain to him more specially, according to that nature which he has in common with other animals: and in virtue of this inclination, those things are said to belong to the natural law, 'which nature has taught to all animals' such as sexual intercourse, education of offspring and so forth."

[147] *Summa Theologiae* I-II, Q. 94, A. 2.

As we saw, Cicero very much focuses upon our rational nature, as when he asks the rhetorical question "what is more divine, I will not say in man only, but in all heaven and earth, than reason?"[148] However, Cicero emphasizes that reason makes us social beings rather than being simply a way of acquiring abstract knowledge. Most of *On the Laws* and *On Duties* is be devoted to developing rules of conduct based on human nature understood as essentially social.

Cicero's and Thomas Aquinas's versions of natural thus seen to be generally compatible, with one major reservation. Cicero does not attempt, nor is he convinced it is possible, to preface his treatment of natural law with a robust demonstration of the existence of God and divine providence. Rather, natural law stands on its own as the best explanation for our actual experience of human nature and conduct. The existence and general nature of God then emerge as the best explanation for the existence of natural law. If one approaches Cicero with the assumption that he bases his position upon strong theological claims, unnecessary confusion will result.

Cicero and Kant

For further clarification and comparison, we shall now briefly consider Immanuel Kant's view of the nature of morality. Like Cicero, Kant often writes about a universal moral law, which he calls the categorical imperative. His initial formulation is that one should "act only on that maxim whereby thou canst at the same time will that it should become a universal law."[149]

---

[148] *On the Laws* 1.22.

[149] Immanuel Kant, *Grounding for the Metaphysics of Morals*, trans. Thomas Kingsmill Abbot (London: Longmans, Green and Co., 1895), par. 421.

Like Cicero, Kant considers that a true moral law must be universal. However, the differences between them are striking. Cicero, as we have seen, seeks to discover this natural law by looking at human nature, as when he states that "we must explain the nature of Justice, and this must be sought for in the nature of man."[150] Kant explicitly rejects such an assumption, for instance when he states in his preface that "the basis of obligation must not be sought in the nature of man, or in the circumstances in the world in which he is placed."[151] That is, he rejects taking human nature or circumstances as the criteria of morality. Rather, moral guidance must be sought "a priori simply in the conception of pure reason."[152] Kant does not wish to rely on an analysis of human nature because he is looking for absolute necessity and certitude which he considers that empirical observations fail to achieve. Thus, he objects that "with what right could we bring into unbounded respect as a universal precept for every rational nature that which perhaps holds only under the contingent conditions of humanity?"[153] For Kant, a truly universal moral law cannot just be based on any particular type of rational being, it must derive from rationality itself.

It is significant that Kant will not use the term *natural law* when describing moral law. His treatment does not take as its starting point a particular nature, human nature, but what follows from rationality itself.

---

https://www.gutenberg.org/ebooks/5682 [accessed July 29, 2021] Paragraph numbers are standard for Kant's works, but are not found in the online text.

[150] *On the Laws* 1.17.

[151] Kant, par. 389.

[152] Kant, par. 389.

[153] Kant, par 408

Hence, it must apply to any rational being. Kant further manifests this point in his distinction between heteronomy and autonomy. This distinction is essential for Kant. Heteronomy means acting for some motive besides that of pure duty. This could be happiness or the will of God. In contrast, autonomy means acting purely from the motive of doing one's duty. He explains that "autonomy of the will is that property of it by which it is a law to itself...The principle of autonomy then is: Always so to choose that the same volition shall comprehend the maxims of our choice as a universal law."[154] One who acts autonomously is motivated only by universal law itself. Only by being autonomous can the will truly be free.[155] He will go further and state that "autonomy then is the basis of the dignity of human and of every rational nature."[156]

Kant would target Cicero's emphasis on acting well as perfecting our rational natures. As we shall see in the next chapter, the whole of the *Dream of Scipio* that concludes Cicero's *On the Republic* is effused with the theme of rewards and punishments for acting well or badly. For Kant, this is the essence of heteronomy. In fact, he considers the principle of seeking happiness as the "most objectionable"[157] moral principle:

> Because the springs it provides for morality are such as rather undermine it and destroy its sublimity, since they put the motives to virtue and to vice in the same class and only teach

---

[154] Kant, par. 440.

[155] Kant, par. 453-454.

[156] Kant, par. 436.

[157] Kant, par. 442.

us to make a better calculation, the specific difference between virtue and vice being entirely extinguished.[158]

According to Kant, this reasoning means that any intrinsic difference between virtue and vice is denied. Both are viewed simply as means to ends. This issue will be considered in the next chapter.

Furthermore, moral law plays a different role in Cicero's ethical thought than in that of Kant. For Cicero, as for Aquinas, a consultation of human nature provides a starting point for making conclusions regarding good or bad actions. For him the emphasis is on recognizing what is the good life for a social being. In contrast, Kant's categorical imperative provides only a negative check on proposed actions. He does not begin with the categorical imperative and derive a list of acceptable actions. Rather, as particular actions are contemplated, they are judged as to whether or not they satisfy the conditions of the categorical imperative. Kant will not even argue that we are necessarily social beings. This position could only be determined negatively by testing cases of antisocial behavior using the categorical imperative.

One of Kant's best-known illustrations is that of keeping promises.[159] Someone may be in a situation of distress where they may consider making a promise without any intention of keeping it. Kant would evaluate the situation by turning to the categorical imperative and asking whether or not this principle of action, making false promises in a state of necessity, could be made a universal rule for all rational beings. He concludes that it could not be done. For, he claims,

---

[158] Kant, par. 442.

[159] Kant discusses this example in *Grounding for the Metaphysics of Morals*, paragraphs 402 and 422.

"I presently become aware that while I can will the lie, I can by no means will that lying should be a universal law."[160] What it means is that I may want to lie myself, but I expect that others will be truthful. If it were a universal law that anyone could make a false promise in a difficult situation, then no one would take my promise seriously. Therefore, this situation fails the test of the categorical imperative. We see that Kant does not base his rejection on human nature and the demands of social life. Rather, the criteria are that it would be contradictory for a rational agent to will to act in this way.

Cicero's approach to evaluating of the same situation would have differed markedly. For him, our turning to our rational and social nature would provide a starting point. Cicero would hold that because we are social and thus, we should act in a way that maintains sociability and avoids actions such as breach of promise, to lie under these circumstances would be contrary to our nature. Cicero's approach is fundamentally teleological. He asks what actions promote human well being. One might characterize the natural law for Cicero as a positive principle from which a conclusion is reached, while Kant's categorical imperative is a negative principle that is used to accept or reject proposed courses of action. Kant would reject this approach as being based on results, not the intrinsic nature of the action. This point of disagreement will be explored more thoroughly in the next chapter.

Kant gives two additional versions of the categorical imperative that might be briefly worth considering in comparison with Cicero's position. Kant's second formulation is that one should "act as to treat humanity, whether in thine own person or in that of any other, in every

---

[160] Kant, par. 403.

case as an end withal, never as means only."[161] This second version centers on the dignity of each person as being ends in themselves. Kant contrasts persons, which have dignity, with everything else which merely has a value: "Whatever has a value can be replaced by something else which is equivalent; whatever, on the other hand, is above all value, and therefore admits of no equivalent, has a dignity."[162] A pen has a value because another one of the same type could adequately replace it. A person, however, Kant considers to not be so replaceable.

One may find a suggestion of the dignity of human beings in *On the Laws*. Cicero in the first book comments that "he who knows himself will realize, in the first place, that he has a divine element within him, and will think of his own inner nature as a kind of consecrated image of god; and so he will always act and think in a way worthy of so great a gift of the gods."[163] Although Cicero and Kant seem to agree to some extent on human dignity, there seems to be a somewhat different emphasis. For Kant, the focus is on the other. His concern is with the question of how one regards another rational being. Does one treat them as an end in themselves or merely as a means to an end? For Cicero the focus is clearly on acting according to one's own rational nature. The divine element he writes of is within one's self. It would be contrary to our own nature to act unjustly towards another rational being.

Kant offers a third form of the categorical imperative. This formulation is derived from the view that humans are able to will to legislate universal law. He relates the second and third versions of the

---

[161] Kant, par. 429.

[162] Kant, par. 434.

[163] *On the Laws* 1.59.

categorical imperative by explaining that "a rational being belongs as a member to the kingdom of ends when, although giving universal laws in it, he is also himself subject to these laws. He belongs to it as sovereign when, while giving laws, he is not subject to the will of any other."[164] This third form takes its origin from the rational being as able to act in accordance with, or participate in, rationality. By being in accordance with the law of reason, one may be said to be a legislator of the law. This statement might call to mind Cicero's treatment of human beings are able to share in right reason, which was his second presupposition for the natural law. Kant certainly goes further than Cicero in regarding rational beings as potentially co-legislators. However, it does not seem that Cicero would necessarily be opposed to this idea.

Conclusion

The comparison of Cicero's position to that of Aquinas and Kant has been intended to clarify his position. We are now ready to return to a further consideration of the role of natural law in Cicero's ethical philosophy. In particular, it has not yet been considered how Cicero explains why one should wish to follow the natural law. This was the question raised by Philus in *On the Republic* 3. To him Laelius had claimed that "whoever is disobedient [to the natural law] is fleeing from himself and denying his human nature, and by reason of this very fact he will suffer the worst penalties, even if he escapes what is commonly called punishment."[165] To this someone might ask, "Why should I care about whether or not I am denying my human nature?" Or to express

---

[164] Kant, par. 433.

[165] *On the Republic* 3.33.

the question in another way: What is the motivation or incentive for following the natural law? Cicero's answer to this question will be explored in the next chapter.

CHAPTER V
The Motivation for Ethical Conduct: The Dream of Scipio

As has been shown in the previous chapter, Cicero conceives justice as deriving from the natural law. But why should one follow the natural law? That is the question to be considered in the present chapter. The questioning of Philus and Laelius's attempt to respond to his claims about the desirability of justice gave impetus and direction to the discussion in Cicero's *On the Republic*. Cicero will provide a resolution to this investigation at the end of the work. But the way he goes about doing so may strike the reader as rather surprising. At the conclusion of a standard philosophical treatise, one would expect to end with a straightforward argument that would give a clear and direct answer to opposing positions. However, Cicero does not provide a conventionally structured argument, but ends with a story.

In ending his dialogue this way he follows his model, Plato's *Republic*, which also ends with a story, the Myth of Er.[166] In Cicero's *On*

---

[166] The Myth of Er is found at the end of Plato's *Republic* at X.614b-621d. Plato also makes use of myths in other dialogues, notably in *Phaedo*, *Gorgias*, and *Phaedrus*.

the Republic the concluding tale is referred to as the *Dream of Scipio* (*Somnium Scipionis*).[167] The Dream seems to be intended, as does the corresponding tale at the end of Plato's *Republic*, as a summation and final argument to the work.[168] Analyzing the key points of the Dream will reveal how Cicero ultimately answers Philus's claim that justice is not desirable for its own sake but merely as a means to an end. Particularly important for understanding Cicero's response will be a consideration of the honorable or noble, which is a good sought for its own sake. The next sections will summarize and analyze the most relevant parts of the Dream.

The *Dream of Scipio*

The Dream is introduced into the discussion by Scipio Aemelianus. He relates to his friends that he experienced this dream at the beginning of the Third Punic War between the Romans and the Carthaginians.[169] For Romans of Cicero's day, the war with Carthage

---

[167] Cicero's *Dream of Scipio* is at *On the Republic* 6.9-29. For a discussion of the background and influence of the *Dream of Scipio*, see C. S. Lewis, *The Discarded Image: An Introduction to Medieval and Renaissance Literature* (Cambridge: Cambridge UP, 1964), 23-28; Frank Ernest Rockwood, "The Somnium Scipionis: Introduction," in *Cicero's Tusculan Disputations, I and Scipio's Dream* (1903; repr., Norman: Oklahoma UP, 1966), iii-x; J. G. F. Powell, "Somnium Scipionis: Introduction," in *Cicero: Laelius, on Friendship and the Dream of Scipio* (Oxford: Aris & Phillips, 1990), 119-133.

[168] Although Plato never directly provides an explanation for his procedure, it is plausible that he was sensitive to the power of a memorable story to convey his meaning that a more straightforward discourse would lack. This explanation would also be in keeping with Plato's making use of the dialogue form in his works in preference to writing treatises. Furthermore, Cicero writing for a general, non-philosophically trained, audience would certainly see the advantage of concluding with a concrete representation rather than an abstract argument.

[169] The setting for the dream is at the beginning of the Third Punic War in 149 BCE.

was viewed as a life-or-death struggle. Scipio, the destroyer of Carthage, ranked as one of the greatest national heroes of Rome. Hence, Scipio can be taken as an outstanding example of public service and sacrifice. In the Dream, he ascends to the heavenly spheres and encounters his adopted grandfather Scipio Africanus.[170] After predicting Scipio's future, which will involve further service to Rome and a threat to his life,[171] Africanus offers encouragement for Scipio to continue his path of political service:

> All those who have preserved, aided, or enlarged their fatherland have a special place prepared for them in the heavens, where they may enjoy an eternal life of happiness. For nothing of all that is done on earth is more pleasing to that supreme God who rules the whole universe than the assemblies and gatherings of men associated in justice, which are called states.[172]

Not only is civic service a good, Africanus explains, it is in fact the greatest activity in the eyes of the supreme God. Such a course of life leads to eternal happiness. Africanus does not consider the retiring life of intellectual contemplation the highest form of life. Rather, the highest place goes to those engaged in political life.[173] As we have seen, this exhortation is in harmony with Cicero's insistence on our social nature and hence the importance of political life. However, a new

---

[170] To avoid confusion, Scipio Aemilianus will be called simply Scipio and Scipio Africanus will be called Africanus.

[171] *On the Republic* 6.11-12.

[172] *On the Republic* 6. 13.

[173] Cicero discusses under what circumstances he would consider legitimate a life devoted to speculation in *On Duties* 1.71-72.

element is the assertion that those who follow such a way of life "enjoy an eternal life of happiness." Up to this point in the dialogue discussions have focused on this life. But now Africanus relates to Scipio the rewards for the virtuous and the punishments for the wicked in the afterlife.

Scipio, confused by this encounter, wonders if Africanus and others he thought to be dead are actually alive. Africanus gives him the paradoxical answer that: "surely all those are alive…who have escaped from the bondage of the body as from a prison; but that life of yours, which men so call, is really death."[174] The dead are truly alive, and the living are dead, so Africanus tells Scipio. The thrust of this paradox is a re-evaluation of the status of life on earth. In conventional thought death is a terrible evil that brings an end to the good of being alive. In the dream, Africanus is declaring that, on the contrary, death does not bring an end to a great good. Rather, the true good life is to be found after death. Hence the afterlife is the true life.[175]

If this is the case, Scipio reasons, then would not the logical course of action be to commit suicide so one could more quickly come to this true life. Africanus is adamantly opposed to this suggestion:

> For unless that God, whose temple is everything that you see, has freed you from the prison of the body, you cannot gain entrance there. For man was given life that he might inhabit that sphere called Earth, which you can see in the centre of this temple; and he has been given a soul out of those eternal fires

---

[174] *On the Republic* 6.14.

[175] An obvious target for Cicero would have been the Epicurean philosophers who denied any future life.

which you call stars and planets…Wherefore you, Publius,[176] and all good men, must leave the soul in the custody of the body, and must not abandon human life except at the behest of him by whom it was given you, lest you appear to have shirked the duty imposed upon you by God.[177]

Africanus' objection derives from the understanding that there is an order of the universe that it would be wrong to disrupt. Scipio has a responsibility to remain alive as part of a larger plan for the universe, even though his personal wish, at this point, might be to die. It is intriguing that Africanus refers to the entire universe as a temple. This way of describing the universe attributes to those who attend to its well being, such as Scipio, the performance of sacred functions. Africanus is thus blurring the distinction between secular and religious activity. Africanus reiterates that Scipio should "imitate your grandfather here; imitate me, your father; love justice and duty, which are indeed strictly due to parents and kinsmen, but most of all to the fatherland. Such a life is the road to the skies."[178]

Furthermore, Africanus identifies the soul as coming from the 'eternal fires' of the stars and planets. Thus the soul is of greater dignity than anything on earth. Cicero will return to this theme in *On the Laws* where he will state that: "he who knows himself will realize, in the first place, that he has a divine element within him, and will think of his own inner nature as a kind of consecrated image of God."[179]

---

[176] Scipio's full name is Publius Cornelius Scipio Aemilianus Africanus Minor.

[177] *On the Republic* 6.15.

[178] *On the Republic* 6.16.

[179] *On the Laws* 1.59.

In the Dream, Scipio looks around him and sees he is surrounded by light. Gazing towards the other spheres he sees that "all else appeared wonderfully beautiful."[180] Turning towards the earth, he sees that the earth and Rome are of small importance compared to the glory of the heavens and observes that "the earth itself seemed to me so small that I was scornful of our empire, which covers only a single point, as it were, upon its surface."[181] Africanus chides Scipio for his excessive attention to the earth and bids him survey the heavens around him. Africanus proceeds to point out the spheres of the planets, finally drawing his attention to the lowest sphere, that of the moon, below which "there is nothing except what is mortal and doomed to decay, save only the souls given to the human race by the bounty of the gods, while above the Moon all things are eternal."[182] Africanus further explains to him the cause and nature of the music of the spheres.[183]

But despite all the wonders he is experiencing, Scipio's gaze returns to the Earth. Africanus bids him consider that "if it seems small to you, as it actually is, keep your gaze fixed upon these heavenly things, and scorn the earthly. For what fame can you gain from the speech of men, or what glory that is worth the seeking?"[184] All human greatness should seem trivial in comparison to the grandeur of the heavens. Furthermore, fame is limited to a small part of the earth. Even if Scipio should be hailed by the Roman people, still many parts of the globe

---

[180] *On the Republic* 6.16.

[181] *On the Republic* 6.16.

[182] *On the Republic* 6.17.

[183] *On the Republic* 6.18-19.

[184] *On the Republic* 6.20.

will never have heard his name.[185] Even the fame that one may achieve will be forgotten by future generations; hence fame is not even long lasting, let alone eternal.[186] Hence Africanus counsels:

> Consequently, if you despair of ever returning to this place, where eminent and excellent men find their true reward, of how little value, indeed, is your fame among men, which can hardly endure for the small part of a single year? Therefore, if you will only look on high and contemplate this eternal home and resting place, you will no longer attend to the gossip of the vulgar herd or put your trust in human rewards for your exploits. *Virtue herself, by her own charms, should lead you on to true glory.*[emphasis added] [187]

Scipio is told to reconsider the scale of importance. Fame should not be considered the highest reward for service, for it is always limited and fleeting. Rather, virtue must be its own reward. An important phrase for interpreting Africanus, and the meaning of the Dream, is Africanus' statement that "virtue herself, by her own charms, should lead you on to true glory." This will be explored in a later section of this chapter.

Scipio is again reminded that that his soul is immortal and that its proper home is the celestial realm:

> Strive on and be sure that it is not you that is mortal, but only your body...know then that you are a god, if a god is that which lives, feels, remembers, and foresees, and which rules,

---

[185] *On the Republic* 6.20-22.

[186] *On the Republic* 6.23.

[187] *On the Republic* 6.25.

governs, and moves the body over which it is set, just as the supreme God above rules this universe....[188]

The special activities of the soul indicate that it is not truly mortal, as are things below the level of the moon, but really belongs to the incorruptible realm. Africanus also makes a parallelism between the soul and God. As God rules and directs the universe, so the soul rules and directs the body. Perhaps Africanus is further implying that as God rules and orders the whole universe, the soul is meant to rule and order its part of the lower universe.

At the end of the dream, Africanus recapitulates the lesson Scipio should have learned. He reminds Scipio that:

> The best tasks are those undertaken in defense of your native land; a spirit occupied and trained in such activity will have a swifter flight to this, its proper home and permanent abode. And this flight will be still more rapid if, while still confined to the body, it looks abroad, and, by contemplating what lies outside itself, detaches itself as much as may be from the body. [189]

Curiously, Scipio is told to engage in public activity while detaching himself from the body. Public service should not be sought for transitory rewards such as wealth or fame, but from a love of nobler things. In contrast, those who follow the lower path and act unjustly are punished:

---

[188] *On the Republic* 6.26.

[189] *On the Republic* 6.29.

For the spirits of those who are given over to sensual pleasure and have become their slaves, as it were, and who violate the laws of gods and men at the instigation of those desires which are subservient to pleasure—their spirits after leaving their bodies fly about close to the earth, and do not return to this place except after many ages of torture.[190]

After his final exhortation, Africanus departs and Scipio awakens. This is also the end of *On the Republic* as we currently have it. Probably this is how Cicero himself ended the work. Plato's *Republic* ends equally abruptly. As Jonathan Powell comments, "What more could Laelius and the rest have said after this?"[191]

Interpreting the Dream

This is the basic story of the *Dream*. How does it provide a solution to the main question of the *On the Republic*? In particular, how does it illuminate Laelius's claim that "whoever is disobedient [to the natural law] is fleeing from himself and denying his human nature, and by reason of this very fact he will suffer the worst penalties, even if he escapes what is commonly called punishment."[192] As we have seen, Africanus emphasises to Scipio the rewards for the virtuous and the punishments for the wicked. One who lives wickedly is "fleeing from

---

[190] *On the Republic* 6.29.

[191] Jonathan Powell, "Explanatory Notes," in *The Republic and The Laws* by Niall Rudd. (Oxford: Oxford UP, 1998), 198 n94.

[192] *On the Republic* 3.33.

himself" by turning from his or her true good to a course of action that is actually harmful.

On an initial reading, Africanus might be thought to be espousing a form of what would today be identified as utilitarianism or consequentialism.[193] Scipio is told to perform certain actions, serving and promoting the benefit of Rome, in return for a reward: a state of happiness after death. This viewpoint is Neal Wood's reading of Cicero's ethics in his aforementioned *Cicero's Social and Political Thought*.[194] There he observes that "possibly Cicero is, among other considerations, trying to appeal to the obvious egoism of his contemporaries, by demonstrating that the way of morality is the pursuit of an enlightened self-interest."[195] This viewpoint is essentially the position of Philus, that just actions are ultimately done for our own benefit. Wood later interprets Cicero's theory of natural law as being rather self-serving. He holds that "a healthy egoism is ever the condition of a wise and prudent altruism, or so Cicero seems to suggest."[196] That is to say, one looks out for the well being of others because it is to one's own advantage. If this interpretation of the Dream

---

[193] Utilitarianism is often considered a species of consequentialism. For the present purposes utilitarianism and consequentialism will not be sharply distinguished. For a discussion of consequentialism and its varieties see *Stanford Encyclopedia of Philosophy*, s.v. "Consequentialism," http://plato.stanford.edu/entries/consequentialism/ (accessed June, 2021).

[194] Wood particularly makes this claim in reference to *On Duties* 2.40 where Cicero gives examples of the usefulness of justice even among thieves. However, his comments are even more relevant to the advantages Africanus attributes to justice in the *Dream of Scipio*.

[195] Wood, 75.

[196] Wood, 77-78.

is correct, Cicero would indeed be simply espousing a form of consequentialism.

According to this reading, Scipio is being told that the advantages of the result, eternal happiness and glory, exceed the negative factors involved in devoting his life to civic activity. Acting virtuously is not even, according to Wood, suggested to be intrinsically desirable. Hence, it seems, Cicero's response to Philus would appear to be that justice is desirable because it will always give greater benefits than injustice. Hence Wood believes that "Cicero never instructs us to abjure self-interest, but only to act as reasonable human beings, pursuing our own advantage in an enlightened and moderate manner, ever mindful of the possible consequences of our conduct."[197]

Wood seems to have a strong case. But if this interpretation is correct, then Cicero is effectively admitting that Philus's argument is unanswerable. It would be hard to explain why Cicero bothered to write the dialogue at all, at least not in the form he did. How is this consideration of rewards and punishments to be reconciled with Cicero's insistence that there are some goods that truly are ends in themselves rather than simply means? A consequentialist reading of the Dream seems to preclude the existence of any such good.

This sense of conflict is deepened if we turn from his *On the Republic* to his *On the Laws*, written at essentially the same time,[198] where we find:

---

[197] Wood, 75-76.

[198] As indicated in Chapter 1, *On the Republic* is generally dated 54-51 BCE, and *Laws* 52-51 BCE.

If it be true that virtue is sought for the sake of other benefits and not for its own sake, there will be only one virtue, which will most properly be called a vice. For in proportion as anyone makes his own advantage absolutely the sole standard of all his actions, to that extent he is absolutely not a good man; therefore *those who measure virtue by the reward it brings believe in the existence of no virtue except vice.* [emphasis added][199]

Here Cicero strongly condemns the suggestion that virtuous conduct is based on self-interest. Rather, virtue requires that an action be done to some extent prescinding from one's own advantage. However, Cicero's position should not be interpreted in a Kantian sense that virtuous actions must be contrary to one's own advantage. Cicero only condemns the idea that self-interest be "absolutely the sole standard" of actions.

Although in the above passage Cicero is strongly anti-consequentialist, nevertheless in Africanus' exhortation the reward seems to be an important component. Cicero seems to be presenting conflicting accounts of why justice should be done. If Cicero is to be taken seriously, there must be some way this discrepancy can be resolved. Even Wood observes that Cicero's position is not as straightforward as it initially appeared to be and admits that "although Cicero believes that morality in the form of justice is advantageous and expedient, at the same time he maintains that it is always in our interest, no matter how unlikely it may seem, to act in a self denying and altruistic fashion."[200] The "no matter how unlikely" caveat calls Wood's line of interpretation into serious question. For some of

---

[199] *On the Laws* 1.49.

[200] Wood, 75.

Cicero's descriptions of motivation seem quite unlikely indeed if one wants to see him as espousing enlightened self-interest as the motivation for virtuous conduct.

Perhaps the difficulty arises from an attempt to shoehorn Cicero into the compartments of modern ethical theories where he does not easily fit. As Walter Nicgorski observes, "the case of Cicero simply brings out in the open a difficulty in distinguishing utilitarianism from classical political thought."[201] These puzzles should lead one to consider the deeper issue as to what Cicero thinks the true motivation for virtue is.

To clarify Cicero's position, it will be worth considering how Cicero's position differs from conventional utilitarianism or consequentialism, although in some ways resembling it. For Cicero's position does indeed appear similar to utilitarianism. In both cases, certain behavior is claimed to result in desirable results. But, insofar as the classical utilitarians often proudly admit that their ethical theory is derived from Epicurus,[202] it would be surprising if such an overt critic of Epicureanism as Cicero should turn out to be himself a utilitarian.

Perhaps the key phrase to unlock Cicero's meaning is an admonition given by Africanus to Scipio that "virtue herself, by her own charms, should lead you on to true glory."[203] What does it mean for virtue to draw by her own charms? As we have seen, Cicero takes as a fundamental principle of ethics that there are goods that are sought

---

[201] Walter Nicgorski, "Cicero's Paradoxes and His Idea of Utility," *Political Theory* 12:4 (Nov, 1984): 573.

[202] John Stuart Mill admits this in the second chapter of *Utilitarianism*. See John Stuart Mill, *Utilitarianism* (1863; repr., Mineola, NY: Dover, 2007), 6-7.

[203] *On the Republic* 6.25.

for their own sake and not just as means to other things. Cicero has no room for an infinite regression of goals. If asked, why should I seek the good, Cicero answers because it is good. To ask for a further reason is to fail to understand the nature of the good. Many philosophers might find agreement with this principle. The point of disagreement would be as to what is the nature of the good that is sought for its own sake. For Cicero, the goods that are sought for their own sake are the noble or honorable, the honorable being "that which is of such a nature that, though devoid of all utility, it can justly be commended in and for itself, apart from any profit or reward."[204]

How does this idea manifest itself in the *Dream of Scipio*? In the Dream, Scipio looks around him and sees he is surrounded by light. Gazing towards the other spheres he sees that "all else appeared wonderfully beautiful."[205] Turning towards the earth, he sees that the earth and Rome are of small importance compared to the glory of the heavens. So, he concludes that "the earth itself seemed to me so small that I was scornful of our empire, which covers only a single point, as it were, upon its surface."[206] Scipio in this passage is not motivated by self-interest, at least not as the term is ordinarily understood. His contemplation of the heavens will not make him wealthier, nor will it increase his prestige and political power. Nor will it provide him with physical security or comfort. Rather, Cicero indicates, the contemplation of the heavens is desired for its own sake. This experience more closely resembles the appreciation of the beautiful

---

[204] *On Ends* 2.45.

[205] *On the Republic* 6.16.

[206] *On the Republic* 6.16.

than the seeking of a utilitarian benefit. This feature is what characterizes the true good for Cicero.

This relationship of the good to the beautiful or the noble is explained by Peter Philips Simpson in this way:

> Such inner harmony or proportion to reason is what Cicero call *honestum* and his Greek predecessors *kalon*, and what we, in imitation of them, may call *the beautiful* or *the noble*. All other goods, as in particular life, health, wealth, fame, and so on, are for the sake of the beautiful and the noble and are only good, strictly speaking, insofar as they serve the beautiful and the noble.[207]

Actions and outcomes may be considered as beautiful and noble. Hence they are goods that are sought for themselves even if no further benefits result from them. Cicero also considers a good soul to be beautiful and noble as well.[208] Injustice is actually not useful because it harms the soul by deflecting it from the true good of acting in accordance with right reason. The benefits from injustice are thus apparent rather than real. Since the good of the soul is to be in harmony with the cosmic order, justice turns out to be always useful because it is for the benefit of the soul. Thus acting justly (or virtuously) as the right ordering of the soul, is intrinsically desirable. Virtue is therefore an end, not just a means. Cicero makes this point in his *On the Laws* where he bluntly states that "if virtue is sought on account of other

---

[207] Peter Phillips Simpson, "Justice, Consequences, and Cicero," in *Vices, Virtues, and Consequences: Essays in Moral and Political Philosophy*, (Washington, D.C.: CUA Press, 2001), 88.

[208] *On the Republic* 6.26.

advantages, there must necessarily be something better than virtue."[209] That is to say if virtue is not an end in itself, but only a means to a further end, what could that further end be? Cicero rhetorically asks:

> Is it money, then, or public office, or beauty, or health? But these things amount to very little when we possess them, and we can have no certain knowledge as to how long they will remain with us. Or is it—the very mention of such a thing is shameful—is it pleasure? But it is precisely in scorning and repudiating pleasure that virtue is most clearly distinguished.[210]

Making virtue a means requires something else to be the end. And nothing else is as good as the wellbeing of the soul, which is found in virtue. As Simpson comments, "to prefer the results of virtuous acts to those acts themselves is to prefer what is lower to what is higher."[211] Virtue itself must be its own reward, otherwise there is no true end.

Therefore, public service should not be sought for transitory rewards such as wealth or fame, but from a love of nobler things. In contrast, Africanus tell Scipio, those who follow the lower path and act unjustly are punished:

> For the spirits of those who are given over to sensual pleasure and have become their slaves, as it were, and who violate the laws of gods and men at the instigation of those desires which are subservient to pleasure—their spirits after leaving their

---

[209] *On the Laws* 1.52.

[210] *On the Laws* 1.52.

[211] Simpson, 89.

bodies fly about close to the earth, and do not return to this place except after many ages of torture.[212]

It is noteworthy that there is no explicit statement that another being is responsible for giving rewards or inflicting punishments. Rather, the soul itself seems to be drawn according to the habits it developed in life. Virtue brings about its own rewards and vice creates its own punishment.[213] This conclusion illuminates Laelius's claim in the *On the Republic* that "whoever is disobedient [to the natural law] is fleeing from himself and denying his human nature, and by reason of this very fact he will suffer the worst penalties, even if he escapes what is commonly called punishment."[214] One who lives wickedly is "fleeing from himself" by turning from his or her true good to a course of action that is actually harmful.

Cicero, Consequentialism, and Deontology

Perhaps a major source of confusion in understanding Cicero's position is the perennial tendency to view ethical theories as one of two extremes: consequentialist ethics where advantages are all important, and deontological ethics where any self-interest or advantage is eschewed. Cicero falls into neither extreme. He rejects the position that only advantage is relevant to decision making and action, for some actions are intrinsically worth doing regardless of outcome. Cicero's approach is that the actions are themselves an end. A just action is in

---

[212] *On the Republic* 6.29.

[213] Powell (*Somnium*, 165) notes that Cicero takes this idea from Plato's *Phaedo* 81c.

[214] *On the Republic* 3.33.

itself a good end. Simpson expresses the resemblance between Cicero's position and consequentialism by noting that:

> One could, accordingly, change virtue ethics into consequentialism and consequentialism into virtue ethics simply by changing what it is that is to be maximized: either from acts to the results of acts, or from the result of acts to acts. To locate the difference between consequentialist theories and virtue theories, one must ignore the strategy of maximizing (for that is common to both) and focus instead on the different things they maximize.[215]

Cicero's position resembles consequentialism in judging actions by outcomes. But the outcomes he wants to maximize are virtuous actions. No amount of other good outcomes takes preference over virtue. In consequentialism, the outcomes are what are attended to. Virtue is only one type of good among others. But for Cicero, virtue, the good of the soul, is not commensurable with any other type of good. For a consequentialist, virtue and other goods are, in theory at least, commensurable. Hence John Stuart Mill can say that "virtue, according to the utilitarian doctrine, is not naturally and originally part of the end, but it is capable of becoming so."[216] Cicero would deny this assertion vehemently. He would assert just the opposite, that virtue is naturally and necessarily part of the human end. So despite certain similarities, these two positions are ultimately quite different.

An example used by Alasdair MacIntyre may perhaps illuminate Cicero's position. In his 1981 work *After Virtue*, he considers the game

---

[215] Simpson, 87-88.

[216] Mill, 31.

of chess.[217] One could encourage a young person to learn chess and to win by offering candy for playing, with a bonus for winning the game. But if getting candy is the child's only motivation, there is no reason for him or her not to cheat. The end is all important, and means are only valuable insofar as they are effective in winning. But if the child, at some stage, comes to enjoy the game in and of itself, he or she will only want to win according to the rules. Enjoying the good of the activity, playing chess well and winning by following the rules, becomes an end sought for itself. Winning the candy or receiving recognition for being a good chess player may still be viewed as desirable, but not at the expense of acting wrongly by cheating. In Cicero's case, there is no way to cheat. The end is essentially connected to, and attained in the performance of, the means. In terms of MacIntyre's example, the end of playing chess well is attained, and is only obtainable, by the means of playing chess well.

But although Cicero cannot be strictly classified as a consequentialist, neither should he be considered a deontologist. Against deontological theories he would be equally adamant that these intrinsically choice-worthy actions will also be beneficial in terms of the good of the soul. Cicero does not accept that there is a radical conflict between seeking good outcomes and acting virtuously (which means acting in accordance with nature). For him, these two options are essentially connected. Acting virtuously will bring the best outcome, doing the good. And the best outcome is the result of acting virtuously. Hence, in *On the Laws* Cicero refers to a statement attributed to Socrates

---

[217] Alasdair MacIntyre, *After Virtue* (Notre Dame: University of Notre Dame Press, 1981), 88.

that he was right to "curse the man who first separated self-interest (*utilitatas*) from justice."[218] Utility and justice are not two unconnected realities. What is just is most useful, and what is most useful is justice. However, utility is understood as the true good, that of the soul and the order of the universe, not as an apparent good. For Cicero, it is not a question of my good *or* the good of others, but seeking the good of *both* myself *and* others. For both a consequentialist and a deontologist, there is a possibility of conflict between the good and my own good. Cicero does not admit this conflict as a real possibility.

Summary

As was discussed in Chapter 3, Cicero thinks that there is a natural law whose existence is discoverable by human reason. By analyzing the nature of reality, one can reach some conclusions about what is in harmony with the nature of things, and hence is good. This present chapter has addressed the question as to what is the motivation for acting in accordance with natural law. Cicero's conclusion is that the good itself can be the only true motivation.

Cicero characterized justice as not an imposition or limitation on human behavior, but rather as flowing from human nature itself. Thus, he will argue that being just is actually the true good of the soul, and injustice is harmful. Hence, he will connect individual good to the good of society as a whole. It may not be too much to say that the more fully developed ethical treatment in *On the Laws, On Ends*, and *On Duties* is an expansion of the themes contained within the *Dream of Scipio*.

---

[218] *On the Laws* 1.33. See *On Duties* 3.11.

How Cicero develops these themes in *On Duties* will be the topic for the next two chapters of the present work. The first book of *On Duties* treats the honorable in itself. From the honorable flow various duties (*officium*). Cicero will consider duties under the four cardinal virtues of wisdom, justice, courage and temperance. Although Cicero considers all four cardinal virtues as relating to the honorable, he gives a special emphasis to justice. These topics will be examined in the next Chapter.

Following those considerations, Cicero turns in Book 2 of *On Duties* to consider things that are useful, especially those things useful for political life. In the third and final book of *On Duties* he considers the possibility of conflict between what is honorable and what is useful. To achieve this objective, he examines examples of the apparent conflict between the useful and the honorable in political life and commercial dealings. The seventh chapter will examine how Cicero carries out this project.

CHAPTER VI
The Honorable and Duties

The treatise *On Duties* occupies a privileged place in the Ciceronian corpus. It is his last, most mature, philosophical work. Unlike the other philosophical writings composed during the last two years of his life, the *On Duties* does not form part of his series of dialogues that provide an overview of Hellenistic philosophy for the Roman reading public. Instead, it is a freestanding work written with a practical end in mind. Cicero dedicated the work to his own son Marcus who had been studying, not terribly diligently, in Athens. Unable due to political conditions to visit his son personally, he offers him guidance in writing. But, although addressed to a particular individual, *On Duties* has relevance for a wider audience, for in it Cicero articulates his ethical vision. Miriam Griffin observes that "*On Duties* is...neither a general tract disguised as a personal address...nor a piece of personal admonition disguised as a general essay...It is both genuinely appropriate to Marcus Cicero and also directed to others, particularly young Romans of the governing class."[219] Hence, *On Duties* is

---

[219] Miriam T. Griffin, Introduction to *Cicero: On Duties*, trans. E. M. Atkins (Cambridge: Cambridge UP, 1991), xvii.

important for understanding how, towards the end of his life, Cicero viewed what it meant to live well. As we have seen, he considers living well to mean living in accordance with our rational nature. In *On Duties* Cicero unpacks his position by examining the obligations that pertain to human beings.

The Meaning of *Officium*

In order to properly understand the *On Duties,* it is necessary to recognize what the title of the work refers to. Duty is, of course, an English term, not a Latin one. The original Latin title of the work is *De Officiis.* Duty is the common translation for the term Cicero uses, *officium.* Cicero in turn employs *officium* to translate the Greek term *kathekon.*[220] This Greek term is used by the Stoic philosophers and carries the sense of "appropriate action."[221] According to classical scholar John M. Cooper in his recent study of ancient philosophy the "term 'appropriate' here is the usual translation of a semi-technical application made by the Stoics…Literally this means 'what comes down on' or is incumbent upon a person, what it is their place to do."[222] What is appropriate depends upon our nature and that of reality as a whole. As Cooper explains further:

---

[220] Later Latin authors universally follow Cicero's translation of *kathekon* as *officium.* Cooper, 202.

[221] Griffin xlv. The meaning of the title and Cicero's translation are discussed more fully in Andrew R. Dyck's *A Commentary on Cicero's De Officiis* (Ann Arbor: U of Michigan Press, 1997), 3-8.

[222] John M. Cooper, *Pursuits of Wisdom: Six Ways of Life in Ancient Philosophy from Socrates to Plotinus* (Princeton: Princeton UP, 2012), 202.

Behind this lies the idea…that nature (or the world-mind, or Zeus) created human beings for a certain sort of life, which is therefore incumbent on us to live (as best we can), as something prescribed to us, as our place in the creation of the world and its developing life over time. By the same token…that life "suits" or "fits" us, and our nature, so that the actions making it up are naturally "appropriate" to us. Hence the normal English rendering of "appropriate acts" is not misleading, even if it does not capture…the etymological connection to duty or obligation.[223]

However, the issue at hand is not how best to translate this term straight from Greek into English. Cicero, obviously, did not write in English. Cicero's task was to determine a suitable Latin term for the Greek term.

Fortunately, Cicero himself explains why he entitled the work as he did. He states that he considers the Latin term *officium* as the proper translation of the Greek term *kathekon*.[224] In his commentary, Andrew R. Dyck discusses the history and meaning of *officium* prior to Cicero's adaptation of the term. He notes, "by Cicero's day the word had undergone a semantic revolution similar to that of *kathekon* prior to its appropriation by Zeno [the founder of Stoicism]."[225] This development was from "reference to an individual's role as a result of a

---

[223] Cooper, 202. The etymological background is discussed more fully in Dyck, *De Officiis*, 4-5.

[224] In a letter to Atticus (XVI.11) he states that: "As to your query about the title, I have no doubt that *kathekon* corresponds with *officium*, unless you have any other suggestion to make." Quotation from: *Letters to Atticus* III, trans. E. O. Winstedt, The Loeb Classical Library 97 (Cambridge, MA: Harvard UP, 1953), 409.

[225] Dyck, *De Officiis*, 6.

given social group," to a broader meaning "beyond social roles to a general moral sense similar to that of *kathekon*."[226] One might characterize this change as the term going from having a social meaning to an ethical meaning.

Therefore, Dyck will state that "in selecting *officium* to render *kathekon* Cicero surely chose the nearest Latin equivalent to the Greek term."[227] In fact:

> Whatever his rendering, however, he would have faced the problem of having to fill it with content derived from Stoic reflection about the nature of the human being and the appropriate action thereby entailed. The problem is not...a divergence in sense of *officium* from *kathekon* per se, but rather the special Stoic sense of *kathekon*, directed toward fulfilling the rational nature of the human being, with *officium* made equivalent by Ciceronian fiat.[228]

Cicero's challenge is to convey the sense of right activity or duty that is based on nature, not social or political convention. Cicero's selection of *On Duties* (*De Officiis*) as the title of his work reveals the unifying thread he will follow:

> For no part of life, neither public affairs nor private, neither in the forum nor at home, neither when acting on your own nor in dealings with another, can be free from duty. Everything

---

[226] Dyck, *De Officiis*, 6.

[227] Dyck, *De Officiis*, 7.

[228] Dyck, *De Officiis*, 7.

that is honourable in a life depends upon its cultivation, and everything dishonourable upon its neglect.[229]

Hence, to understand what is truly honorable, one needs to discover what duties one has. Cicero emphasizes that these duties flow from our nature as rational and, therefore, as social beings.

Different translators and commentators will use diverse terms to convey the meaning of *officium*. Commonly, for translations of Cicero's work into English, *officium* has been rendered as *duty*. Therefore, the work is generally entitled *On Duties* in English translations. Unfortunately, this term can be misunderstood if one interprets it in a Kantian sense. Clarification is perhaps needed.

Cicero, Kant, and Duty

In contemporary philosophical discourse, the mention of duty immediately conjures up thoughts of Kantian ethics. For duty is indeed a cornerstone of Kant's ethical considerations. Appropriately enough, the common term used to refer to his ethical system is Deontology, literally meaning the study of duty. Kant states early on in his *Grounding for the Metaphysics of Morals* that the moral worth of an action depends "not in the purpose that is to be obtained by it, but in the maxim according to which the action is determined."[230] For Kant, the maxim means the motive for action. The only truly good motive, in Kant's view, is one done from duty. Duty he defines

---

[229] *On Duties* 1.4. Cicero, *On Duties*, trans. E. M. Atkins. Cambridge Texts in the History of Philosophy (Cambridge: Cambridge UP, 1991), 3. Unless otherwise noted, all translations of the *On Duties* will be from this translation.

[230] Kant, 2 par. 399.

as acting "out of respect for the law."[231] By law, as was discussed in chapter 4, Kant means not a human made law. Rather, he is referring to the universal law of reason that is expressed as a categorical imperative. A categorical imperative is one that commands absolutely to do or not do some action. In such a case there is no appeal to any end to be achieved such as to be happy or avoid a punishment. Kant describes such an imperative as "one which represented an action as objectively necessary in itself, without reference to another end."[232] A merely hypothetical imperative is one that commands some action as a means to an end such as being happy or avoiding punishment. Kant distinguishes this type of imperative from a categorical imperative by defining a hypothetical imperative as one which presents a possible action "as a means for attaining something else that one wants (or may possibly want)."[233]

How can these Kantian distinctions be applied to Cicero's concept of duty? As was discussed in Chapter 5, his ethical position does not fall neatly into the dominant categories of either consequentialism or deontology. In regards to the current topic, deontologists posit the possibility of a conflict between the good itself and my own personal good. This distinction Cicero does not admit. Although he treats of the natural law explicitly in *On the Laws*, it seems to be misleading to say that Cicero would identify the good man as acting "out of respect for the law." The natural law does not merely give a set of rules to follow, but reveals what rules to

---

[231] Kant, 13 par. 400.

[232] Kant, 25 par. 414.

[233] Kant 25 par. 414.

follow in order to live well. Cicero's position is that duty means not acting exclusively out of respect for law, but to fulfill our human nature as found in individual circumstances. Kant would likely classify Cicero's position as involving hypothetical rather than truly categorical imperatives.

Because of the fundamental difference between Kant and Cicero, the use of duty as a translation could be misleading. Returning to the original Stoic term, Dyck notes that "*kathekon* is a much broader term than 'duty' and can apply even to plants and animals."[234] Kant would certainly not write of plants or animals having duties. His focus is exclusively on rational agents and the grounds of their actions.

At least partially due to this source of confusion, recent translators have sought alternatives to *duty* as a translation of *officium*. P. G. Walsh's recent translation is entitled *On Obligations*.[235] Although in her translation Atkins follows the convention for the title of the book, in the introduction Griffin notes that in some cases a closer translation might be responsibilities.[236] Dyck prefers appropriate action.[237] This last option may be the least confusing translation.

The honorable is found in carrying out appropriate actions. Cicero goes so far as to say that "honorable behavior lies entirely in the performance of such obligations, and likewise base conduct lies

---

[234] Dyck, *De Officiis*, 8.

[235] *Cicero: On Obligations*, trans. P.G. Walsh (Oxford: Oxford UP, 2000). Walsh discusses his reasons for selecting this term on page liv.

[236] Griffin, xlv.

[237] Dyck, *De Officiis*, 8.

in neglecting them."[238] In the last chapter we introduced an important theme, the honorable, that which is an end in itself. Hence, one may view *On Duties* as concretizing the meaning of natural law by drawing out the implications of the natural law for action. Cicero will consider appropriate actions in book 1 of *On Duties* by examining the four cardinal virtues: wisdom, justice, courage, and temperance. The first virtue he will consider is wisdom, which involves "the perception of truth and with ingenuity."[239] The honorable is also found in justice, which is concerned "with preserving fellowship among men, with assigning to each his own, and with faithfulness to agreements one has made."[240] A third source of the honorable is that which involves "the greatness and strength of a lofty and unconquered spirit",[241] which is courage. Finally, a fourth source of the honorable is temperance, which resides in "order and limit in everything that is said and done."[242]

Wisdom

Cicero begins by considering wisdom. This virtue is perhaps the obvious one to begin with if one wants to emphasize our nature as rational beings. He discusses wisdom and the other cardinal virtues in

---

[238] *On Duties* 1.4. Walsh translation.

[239] *On Duties* 1.15.

[240] *On Duties* 1.15.

[241] *On Duties* 1.15.

[242] *On Duties* 1.15.

a striking passage in *On Ends*.[243] His claim is that "nature has also engendered in mankind the desire of contemplating truth. This is most clearly manifested in our hours of leisure; when our minds are at ease we are eager to acquire knowledge even of the movements of the heavenly bodies. This primary instinct leads us to love all truth as such."[244] To be human, Cicero says, is to be a truth-seeking and truth-loving being. Hence one sort of honorable activity is understanding. Cicero affirms in *On Duties* that human beings are essentially 'rational animals' when he comments that:

> We have divided the nature and power of that which is honourable under four headings. The first of these, consisting of the learning of truth, *most closely relates to human nature*. For all of us feel the pull that leads us to desire to learn and know; we think it a fine thing to excel in this, while considering it bad

---

[243] *On Ends* 2.46-47. "Nature has also engendered in mankind the desire of contemplating truth. This is most clearly manifested in our hours of leisure; when our minds are at ease we are eager to acquire knowledge even of the movements of the heavenly bodies. This primary instinct leads us to love all truth as such, that is, all that is trustworthy, simple and consistent, and to hate things insecure, false and deceptive, such as cheating, perjury, malice and injustice. Further, Reason possesses an intrinsic element of dignity and grandeur, suited rather to require obedience than to render it, esteeming all the accidents of human fortunes not merely as endurable but also as unimportant; a quality of loftiness and elevation, fearing nothing, submitting to no one, ever unsubdued. These three kinds of moral goodness being noted, there follows a fourth kind, possessed of equal beauty, and indeed arising out of the other three. This is the principle of order and of restraint. From recognizing something analogous to this principle in the beauty and dignity of outward forms, we pass to beauty in the moral sphere of speech and conduct. Each of the three excellences mentioned before contributes something to this fourth one: it dreads rashness; it shrinks from injuring anyone by wanton word or deed; and it fears to do or say anything that may appear unmanly."

[244] *On Ends* 2.46.

and dishonourable to stumble, to wander, to be ignorant, to be deceived. [emphasis added][245]

Cicero is well aware of the attraction of the life devoted to seeking truth. He would consider anyone who does not feel, to some degree, the attraction to this life to be living in a subhuman way. He goes so far as to comment "if anyone despises the pursuit of [wisdom], it is difficult to see what on earth he would see fit to praise."[246]

However, despite his extolling of rationality, Cicero is adamant that the truly good human life is one in which intellectual pursuits are not allowed to take one away from one's other responsibilities. Such a course of action would be contrary to our social nature.

In particular, Cicero points out two faults those who pursue truth are likely to fall into. Firstly, "we should not take things that have not been ascertained for things that have, and rashly assert them."[247] Both through his political and philosophical experiences, he emphasized the difficulty and often impossibility of attaining certitude. Hence one should be cautious in thinking one has achieved certainty.

The second fault he cautions against "is that some men bestow excessive devotion and effort upon matters that are both abstruse and difficult, and unnecessary."[248] Cicero has a keen sense that human beings should be aware of their limits. We should recognize that with limited time available, certain obligations are more pressing than others. The desire to study obscure and difficult theoretical questions

---

[245] *On Duties* 1.18.

[246] *On Duties* 2.5.

[247] *On Duties* 1.18.

[248] *On Duties* 1.19.

remote from human life and activity is an indulgence that will generally conflict with our other activities and hence be contrary to appropriate action. He will condemn such a course, writing that "when, however those without a reason claim to despise the commands and magistracies which most men admire, I do not think that should be counted as praiseworthy – indeed no, but rather as a vice."[249]

Nevertheless, he does admit there are some situations that would justify one's devoting oneself to a life of intellectual pursuits rather than the active life:

> Men of outstanding ability who have devoted themselves to learning rather than choose public life, or those who have retired from public life hampered by ill health or some quite serious cause, should therefore perhaps be excused when they yield to others the power and praise of governing.[250]

Although Cicero does not make the point explicitly, one might also view those who devote their lives to intellectual pursuits as potentially contributing to a community. He himself exemplified this path when, barred from political activity in the last two years of his life, he devoted his time to making philosophy accessible to his busy countrymen through his writings. Cicero's sending his son to Athens to complete his education also illustrates his view that intellectuals can benefit others.

---

[249] *On Duties* 1.71.

[250] *On Duties* 1.71.

The Relationship of Wisdom and the Moral Virtues

Cicero takes great pains to show how the active virtues flow from wisdom and are essential for a fully human life. His fundamental principle is that, "in my view those duties that have their roots in sociability conform more to nature than those drawn from learning."[251] This statement should not be surprising. He has consistently maintained that the good life is life in community. Cicero rejects the thesis that love of the pursuit of wisdom means a withdrawal from human life. In fact, he will go so far as to say that:

> Suppose that a wise man were granted a life plentifully supplied with everything he needed so that he could, by himself and completely at leisure, reflect and meditate upon everything worth learning. But suppose also that he were so alone that he never saw another man: would he not then depart from life?[252]

Cicero's point is not that such a person would die.[253] Rather, he regards the solitary life as not a truly human life. Such a person would have left behind a truly human life. Rather than viewing the solitary life of thought to be the ideal, he holds that to be wise means to be in

---

[251] *On Duties* 1.153.

[252] *On Duties* 1.153.

[253] Both Walter Miller and P. G. Walsh translate 'excedat e vita' as "he would die." Both Miller and Walsh seem to translate this passage in an overly literal way that is not sensible in the context of what Cicero is discussing. Walsh recognizes this when he comments in a note to this passage that: "Cicero has granted the solitary philosopher 'abundant provision of everything', it is hard to see the justification of this statement. If on the other hand he were dependent on others for life's necessities, the statement would be justified." P. G. Walsh, *Cicero: On Obligations* (Oxford: Oxford UP, 2000), 155. Nevertheless, Walsh does not conclude that Cicero does not mean physical death when he describes such a wise man as departing from life.

accordance with human nature. And being in accordance with human nature means sociability, not just rationality. Perhaps this idea would be better expressed as sociability grounded in rationality. Hence, he will explain, "that wisdom which I have given the foremost place is the knowledge of things human and divine, which is concerned also with the bonds of union between gods and men and the relations of man to man."[254] His position should be clear: because we have knowledge, we know that we have certain duties to our fellow rational beings.

This connection is sometimes missed, resulting in a misunderstanding of Cicero's position. For example, in the notes to the Loeb translation of *On Duties*, Walter Miller claims that "Cicero is guilty of a curious fallacy" by introducing the premise that "'the bonds of union between gods and men and the relations of man to man' are derived from wisdom, and therewith sidetracks wisdom and gives the duties derived from the social instinct the place from which wisdom has been shunted."[255] This interpretation does not take account of the position he developed in *On the Republic* and *On the Laws*, especially in the *Dream of Scipio*, that true wisdom is to recognize the good that is to be pursued. Hence, all practical virtues and duties can be said to be derived from wisdom. Griffin catches this connection when she observes that "wisdom is foremost in the sense that it is basic and directive; it includes the understanding of the cosmic community that is a prerequisite for action."[256] To be wise is to act according to wisdom.

---

[254] *On Duties* 1.153.

[255] Walter Miller, *Cicero: On Duties*. The Loeb Classical Library 30 (Cambridge, MA: Harvard UP, 1913), 156-157.

[256] Griffin, 60. See Walsh, 155-156.

Cicero concludes that wisdom is origin and measure for the other three cardinal virtues. Appropriate actions are wise actions.

Justice

Based on this understanding of the connection between wisdom and the active life, Cicero will explain how the other virtues follow. He situates justice by describing it as comprising "the reasoning by which the fellowship of men with one another, and the communal life, are held together."[257] This connection of reason and justice is also made in *On Ends*, where he indicates how justice flows from our love of truth. He says that "this primary instinct leads us to love all truth as such, that is, all that is trustworthy, simple and consistent, and to hate things insecure, false and deceptive, such as cheating, perjury, malice and injustice."[258] Love of truth is often thought of as love of speculative truth, such as knowledge of physics or metaphysics. Cicero, however, emphasizes that the love of truth includes the truth about the practical order, how one should act and live.

Cicero identifies two fundamental obligations of justice. First, "no man should harm another unless he has been provoked by injustice."[259] The first obligation of justice is the most obvious. One owes it to another not to harm them without cause. No community can function if injury is considered acceptable as a matter of course. Such a condition would likely degenerate into a Hobbesian state of nature.

---

[257] *On Duties* 1.20.

[258] *On Ends* 2.46.

[259] *On Duties* 1.20.

The second obligation is that "one should treat common goods as common and private ones as one's own."[260] Once again, this obligation is one that flows from the very nature of communal life. Without some stability and recognition of private property, anarchy would prevail. The converse of this principle is that genuinely common property should be recognized as such and used for the common welfare. Both private and common properties thus serve and promote the well being of the community.

Cicero is sometimes criticized for an excessive and class-based interest in private property.[261] However, his position is deeper than mere class self interest. He readily admits that the ownership of private property is conventional, such that "no property is private by nature, but rather by long occupation (as when men moved into some empty property in the past), or by victory (when they acquired it in war), or by law, by settlement, by agreement, or by lot."[262] Although recognizing the conventional nature of property, Cicero does not take the step that some other thinkers take and advocate alternative schemes for the distribution of property. Rather, "we ought in this to follow nature as our leader, to contribute to the common stock of the things that benefit everyone together, and, by the exchange of dutiful services, by giving and receiving expertise and effort and means, to bind fast the fellowship of men with

---

[260] *On Duties* 1.20.

[261] For example, Neal Wood in *Cicero's Social and Political Thought*, pages 105-119. For a critique of Wood's thesis, see J. Jackson Barlow, "Cicero on Property and the State," in *Cicero's Practical Philosophy*, ed. Walter Nicgorski (South Bend, Ind: University of Notre Dame Press, 2012), 212-237.

[262] *On Duties* 1.21.

each other."[263] Instead of redistributing or abolishing private property, he advocates a voluntary sharing of benefits.

Cicero introduces a companion to justice, namely beneficence. For him, "there are two parts of this [reasoning]: justice, the most illustrious of the virtues, on account of which men are called 'good'; and the beneficence connected with it, which may be called either kindness or liberality."[264] One might view justice as being minimalistic in the sense of giving someone only what is due to them, whereas beneficence means going further. He is proposing that there is more to social life than doing the minimum of avoiding committing injustice. Rather, our social nature expresses itself in benefiting the fellow members of our community, whether or not we have an obligation to them in the conventional sense of the term. He will even extend the range of beneficence in some degree simply to those who share in human nature, so "if any assistance can be provided without detriment to oneself, it should be given even to a stranger."[265]

Cicero observes that our precise obligations may vary depending upon circumstances. For example, someone who has borrowed something is ordinarily obliged to return it when asked. However, there may be circumstances when this action would be unjust and hence not obligatory.[266] In order to clarify his position, he enunciates two principles when an obligation will not be binding. The first is that

---

[263] *On Duties* 1.22.

[264] *On Duties* 1.20.

[265] *On Duties* 1.51.

[266] Cicero likely has in mind the conversation between Socrates and Cephalus in Republic 331b-d, considered in Chapter 2 above. The item under discussion is a weapon and whether or not it should be returned to one who has lost his mind.

"promises should not be kept if they are disadvantageous to those to whom you have made them."[267] He illustrates this principle by the story of the promise the god Neptune made to Theseus to grant him three wishes.[268] In a fit of anger, Theseus requests the death of his son Hippolytus, which Neptune grants. Later Theseus is deeply grieved by what he has done. In this situation, Cicero maintains, Neptune should not have fulfilled his promise.

In another example, a wise man might have promised to dance in the forum if he was named a rich man's heir.[269] If he judges such an action to be shameful, he should not do it. Either he should not take the money at all, or give the money to the state in the case of a crisis. In the latter case, since it is for the good of the state, Cicero does not consider it shameful to dance in the forum.

His second principle is that "if [the promises] harm you more than they benefit the person whom you have promised, is it contrary to duty to prefer the greater good to the lesser."[270] He gives the example of promising to speak on someone's behalf in the law court. Ordinarily one would have a duty to keep that promise. However, if your son became seriously ill, it would not be unjust to attend to him rather than keep your promise to go to the law court. In fact, Cicero holds, "the person to whom you have made the promise would be failing his duty if he complained that he had been abandoned."[271]

---

[267] *On Duties* 1.32.

[268] The story is told by Euripides in his play *Hippolytus*.

[269] *On Duties* 3.93.

[270] *On Duties* 1.32.

[271] *On Duties* 1.32.

In order to clarify justice, Cicero will discuss the nature of injustice. He will do so by considering two sources of injustice: "Of injustice there are two types: men may inflict injury; or else, when it is being inflicted upon others, they fail to deflect it even though they could."[272] One is unjust by action by positively acting against justice. But one can also be unjust by failing to act. Thus, Cicero does not regard merely refraining from doing harm as making one virtuous. We have social obligations to do the good, not just refrain from doing evil. Furthermore, we have an obligation to prevent harm. He will go so far as to say that "the man who does not defend someone, or obstruct the injustice when he can, is at fault just as if had abandoned his parents or his friends or his country."[273]

Justice is the fundamental virtue of the practical order. Without justice, social life is impossible. Justice makes the other virtues possible, for it "is the sovereign mistress and queen of all the virtues."[274]

To fail to act justly is to fail to carry out one's most essential duties. There are also several motives for failing to act justly:

> For some men do not wish to incur enmities, or toil, or expense; others are hindered by indifference, laziness, inactivity or some pursuits or business of their own, to the extent that they allow people whom they ought to protect to be abandoned."[275]

---

[272] *On Duties* 1.23.

[273] *On Duties* 1.23.

[274] *On Duties* 1.28.

[275] *On Duties* 1.28.

In all these cases, personal concerns are given precedence over the duties required by justice. Cicero will examine this topic when he considers the relationship of the honorable and the useful in the second and third books of *On Duties*. These books will be considered in the next chapter.

Courage

From our rational nature a third virtue follows, namely courage, which Cicero describes as "the greatness and strength of a lofty and unconquered spirit."[276] He provides a fuller explanation of the connection of courage to reason in *On Ends*:

> Reason possesses an intrinsic element of dignity and grandeur, suited rather to require obedience than to render it, esteeming all the accidents of human fortunes not merely as endurable but also as unimportant; a quality of loftiness and elevation, fearing nothing, submitting to no one, ever unsubdued.[277]

Being reasonable leads us to view the vagaries of fortune and the trials of life as much less important than they are generally regarded. Hence, in Cicero's treatment, courage is described as greatness of spirit, which emphasizes that courage means rising above an excessive fear of struggles. A great souled person does not fear battle because they do not consider death the greatest evil. Nor do they shrink from political conflict, because they value the good to be achieved above their own security.

---

[276] *On Duties* 1.15.

[277] *On Ends* 2.46.

Like justice and wisdom, courage also finds its appropriate setting in community. The life of a community is not sustainable if individuals are not willing to face danger for their fellow citizens. The mention of courage generally evokes thoughts of battle and facing other direct threats to one's life. However, Cicero departs from expectations by emphasizing "lofty and unconquered spirit" rather than focusing exclusively on military prowess. [278] He will explain that "most men consider that military affairs are of greater significance than civic; I must deflate that opinion. For men have not infrequently sought war out of desire for glory."[279] Although not denying that military affairs require courage, he considers courage to be better exemplified in civic affairs. Thus, he says, "If we are prepared to judge the matter correctly, many achievements of civic life have proved greater and more famous than those of war."[280] Cicero agrees that military prowess is required for a society to maintain itself. However, without courageous political leaders society would collapse from within.

Cicero will further discuss two ways in which courage can be exhibited. The first "lies in disdain for things external, in the conviction that a man should admire, should choose, should pursue nothing except what is honourable and seemly, and should yield to no man, nor to agitation of the spirit, nor to fortune."[281] The first way has to do with one's attitude to the circumstances one encounters. One may perhaps characterize it as one's interior disposition.

---

[278] *On Duties* 1.15.

[279] *On Duties* 1.74.

[280] *On Duties* 1.74.

[281] *On Duties* 1.66.

The second way is in one's exterior actions. Thus, he maintains, that "you should, in the spirit I have described, do deeds which are great, certainly, but above all beneficial, and you should vigorously undertake difficult and laborious tasks which endanger both life itself and much that concerns life."[282] The outward actions depend upon and exhibit the interior disposition.[283] Courage thus reveals itself in public service as well as in military activity. So he writes that "those who are equipped by nature to administer affairs must abandon any hesitation over winning office and engage in public life. For only in this way can either the city be ruled or greatness of spirit be displayed."[284]

Surprisingly, Cicero considers courage, from one viewpoint, to be most accessible to philosophers. This position becomes intelligible when one considers that "there is less in their life which is vulnerable to the blows of fortune, and their needs are fewer; and if they do meet with misfortune, their fall cannot be so severe."[285] Philosophers experience courage, greatness of soul, because they constantly live lives of detachment from external circumstances. This attitude is more difficult to maintain for those constantly engaged in public activity. Therefore, he can say that statesmen must, even more than philosophers, "acquire the magnificent disdain for human affairs that I stress, and tranquility of mind and freedom from care."[286]

---

[282] *On Duties* 1.66.

[283] *On Duties* 1.67.

[284] *On Duties* 1.72.

[285] *On Duties* 1.73.

[286] *On Duties* 1.72.

Temperance and the Seemly

Finally, Cicero will consider the nature of the virtue of temperance, which he describes as including "a sense of shame and what one might call the ordered beauty of a life, restraint and modesty, a calming of all the agitations of the spirit, and due measure in all things."[287] In *On Ends* Cicero describes temperance as involving elements of the other three cardinal virtues. Temperance "dreads rashness" as does wisdom; it "shrinks from injuring anyone by wanton word or deed" and hence involves justice, and requires courage, viewed as greatness of spirit, because "it fears to do or say anything that may appear unmanly."[288] Negatively, temperance is the virtue that draws back from what is shameful concerning the appetites.[289] Viewed positively, temperance is essentially seeking order in one's life.

Cicero relates temperance to *decorum*. This term is variously translated as propriety, the seemly or the fitting.[290] The nature of decorum is somewhat obscure in Cicero's treatment. Dyck considers the discussion of *decorum* to be "perhaps the most difficult section" in *On Duties*.[291] Among the difficulties is that it seems that "a term from the aesthetic sphere is adapted to ethical uses."[292] That is, in modern discourse, what is fitting or seemly does not typically carry the sense of

---

[287] *On Duties* 1.93.

[288] *On Ends* 2.47.

[289] In distinction from courage, which avoids what is shameful in regards to moderating one's reaction of fear.

[290] Miller in the Loeb translation uses 'propriety'. 'The seemly' is used by Atkins. Walsh makes use of 'the fitting' in his translation.

[291] Dyck, *De Officiis*, 241.

[292] Dyck, *De Officiis*, 241.

moral obligation. However, Walsh notes, even though the fitting is "an aesthetic rather than a moral concept...it is an appropriate criterion of moral behavior."[293] This recalls the point that appropriate actions are broader than what we would consider today as being virtuous. Appropriate actions are those that are, more generally, in accordance with our nature.

Cicero considers *decorum* to be inseparable from the honorable, because "the essence of [*decorum*] is that it cannot be separated from what is honourable: for what is seemly is honourable, and what is honourable is seemly."[294] In fact, their relationship is rather opaque.

Unhelpfully, Cicero is evasive about giving a definition of the seemly, stating, "it is easier to grasp than to explain what the difference is between the 'honourable' and 'seemly'."[295] He posits that the relationship between the honorable and seemly is such that "what is seemly is manifested...when the honorable precedes it."[296] The best initial definition might be P.G. Walsh's explanation that the seemly "is the manifestation of the honourable in action."[297] The seemly can be viewed as the observable actions that flow from an honorable condition or disposition. However, this description seems to apply to all four cardinal virtues. How is the seemly to be distinguished?

There seems to be vagueness, going back to Cicero's Stoic sources, in the relationship of the seemly and virtue as a whole and the seemlys

---

[293] Walsh, 145.

[294] *On Duties* 1.93.

[295] *On Duties* 1.93.

[296] *On Duties* 1.94.

[297] Walsh, 145.

relationship to temperance in particular.[298] On the one hand, the seemly is coextensive with the honorable and is hence applicable to every virtue. In this sense, Cicero claims, that "seemliness of a general kind, [is] involved with honourable behavior as a whole."[299] In this sense, what is seemly is that which agrees with the excellence of man where his nature differs from that of other creatures."[300] Regarding wisdom, "it is seemly to use reason and speech sensibly, to do what one does with forethought, in everything to see and gaze on what is true."[301] The contrary actions that show a lack of wisdom are unseemly, so "on the other hand, mistakes, errors, lapses, misjudgments are as unseemly as delirious insanity."[302] So too, the just is honorable and thus seemly, but injustice is dishonorable and hence unseemly.[303] Thirdly, Cicero will describe seemliness as related to courage, as "what is done in a great and manly spirit seems worthy of a human being and seemly."[304]

Although seemliness applies to all that is honorable, it is particularly applicable to temperance.[305] So in the second sense Cicero will sometimes identify seemliness with temperance. This more limited usage "takes the seemly to be that which agrees with nature in such a way that moderation and restraint appear in it, along with the

---

[298] Dyck, *De Officiis* 242-243. Walsh, 145.

[299] *On Duties* 1.96.

[300] *On Duties* 1.96.

[301] *On Duties* 1.94.

[302] *On Duties* 1.94.

[303] *On Duties* 1.94.

[304] *On Duties* 1.94.

[305] *On Duties* 1.93.

appearance of a gentleman."[306] In this narrower meaning seemliness is identified with moderation in physical appetites, rather than with conduct in general that would fall under the other three virtues. Cicero argues that temperance is in accordance with human nature because we are rational and hence should not allow pleasure to lead us to act unwisely; thus, " bodily pleasure is not sufficiently worthy of the superiority of man and...it should be scorned and rejected."[307] Pleasure is not necessarily an evil, but one should "keep his enjoyment of it in proportion."[308] In concrete terms, Cicero maintains that, "The nourishment and care we give our bodies should therefore be measured by the needs of healthiness and strength, not of pleasure."[309]

Hierarchy of Duties

To summarize, Cicero sees the four cardinal virtues as being the source of the honorable and hence of duties.[310] He concludes the first book of *On Duties* with a brief consideration of the criteria by which obligations deriving from these four sources can be weighed when they conflict and also "to determine which is the more honourable of two honourable courses."[311]

---

[306] *On Duties* 1.96.

[307] *On Duties* 1.106.

[308] *On Duties* 1.106.

[309] *On Duties* 1.106.

[310] *On Duties* 1.152. "Everything that is honourable has its source in the four elements: the first learning, the second sociability, the third greatness of spirit, and the fourth moderation."

[311] *On Duties* 1.152.

As should be clear from his considerations in *On the Republic, On the Laws,* and *On Duties,* Cicero has given priority to justice as the paramount virtue of our nature as social, rational, beings. Hence, the most pressing duties will be the social obligations that flow from justice. Cicero makes his meaning explicit when he states that, "from all this we realize that the duties of justice must be given precedence over the pursuit of knowledge and the duties imposed by that."[312] His intention is not to disparage wisdom, but to view wisdom as being essentially ordered to activity. So he writes, "the wisdom that I declared to be the foremost is the knowledge of all things human and divine; and it includes the sociability and fellowship of gods and men with each other."[313]

Furthermore, among social obligations, a hierarchy exists. In the concrete, "duties are owed first to the immortal gods, secondly to one's country, thirdly to one's parents, and then down the scale to others."[314] Earlier in *On Duties* Cicero had considered our duties to our country and parents as being the greatest because of the greater benefits they have given us.[315] But we also have duties to others, such as our children who need our support and to our neighbors.

However, Cicero is not going to adopt the consequentialist position that one should benefit one's fellows no matter what sort of means are used. Rather, he maintains that "some things are so disgraceful, or so outrageous, that a wise man would not do them even

---

[312] *On Duties* 1.155.

[313] *On Duties* 1.153.

[314] *On Duties* 1.160.

[315] *On Duties* 1.158.

to protect his country... And so a wise man will not undertake them for the sake of the republic, and indeed the republic will not want him to undertake them for its sake."[316] As we have seen in the previous chapter, Cicero will consider dishonorable actions as intrinsically undesirable. Hence, actions fundamentally against our nature should never be done as they act against the end we are seeking. This principle is true not just for individuals, but for society as a whole. For, "a situation could not arise where it would benefit the republic for such a man to perform any such deed."[317] Cicero is reluctant to give any examples, considering it dishonorable even to mention them, but refers readers for a list to a now lost work of the Stoic philosopher Posidonius.

In book 2 of *On Duties* Cicero will add another layer to his discussion by considering useful things such as popularity, money, and health. Finally, in book 3 he will discuss the relationship and possible conflicts between the useful and the honorable. These topics will be considered in the next chapter.

---

[316] *On Duties* 1.159.

[317] *On Duties* 1.159.

CHAPTER VII
The Useful and the Honorable

Cicero, in *On Duties* 1, considered what actions are appropriate for human beings. These appropriate actions, *officium*, were considered under the heading of the four cardinal virtues: wisdom, justice, courage, and temperance. In each case, he attempted to show how virtuous actions were in accordance with our rational, social nature. Furthermore, Cicero drew a connection between appropriate actions and the honorable. Recall that the honorable was characterized as that which is sought for its own sake. The honorable is a good or end in itself and not, or not only, a means to another end. To discover what is honorable one must know what actions one ought to perform. Hence, he will consider, regarding *officium,* that "everything that is honourable in a life depends upon its cultivation, and everything dishonourable upon its neglect."[318]

The Useful

The remainder of the *On Duties* is devoted to a consideration of the useful, that which is sought for something beyond itself, and its

---

[318] *On Duties* 1.4.

relationship to what is honorable. Cicero defines the useful or beneficial as what "is conducive to the advantageousness and pleasantness of life, to opportunities and resources for doing things, to wealth and to power, all of which enable [individuals] to benefit themselves and those dear to them."[319] The useful thus covers many things. Good health and money are useful.[320] Various things or attributes that allow us to engage in desired activities and achieve our goals are useful as well.[321] Whatever is a means to acquiring political support he also considers under this heading of the useful.[322] In keeping with his emphasis on civic life, he devotes the longest portion of his treatment to those things that are conducive to gaining popular support. He will particularly devote a great deal of attention to things useful in gaining popular support by the use of wealth and the giving of service.

Given the emphasis Cicero gives to the useful, one might be puzzled as to the relationship between the useful and the honorable. Marcia L. Colish describes the distinction between the useful and the honorable by stating that "for Cicero the *honestum* as he sees it in the *On Duties* is the common good and the *utile* is individual interest."[323] This is a useful dichotomy. However, it seems a clarification is needed. For, Cicero does affirm that the useful is not just what is to our own benefit. Usefulness also includes what benefits our friends and

---

[319] *On Duties* 1.9.

[320] *On Duties* 2.86-87.

[321] *On Duties* 2.11-15.

[322] *On Duties* 2.21-85.

[323] Colish, 150

associates.[324] Moreover, he had argued that our beneficence should extend to society as a whole, that is, to the common good. One might better make the distinction between what is good for a segment of the community versus the good of the whole community. The useful is what is advantageous to myself and my associates, which may or may not be for the common good. As we shall see, Cicero does not think there can really be a conflict between the useful and the common good.

The Useful and the Good

What does Cicero regard as the moral status of the useful? He finds himself disagreeing with his Stoic sources in how he evaluates the useful. According to Zeno, the founder of Stoicism, those things "which both good and bad use can be made of" cannot be called good.[325] Hence, he limited the good to what is virtuous, "prudence, justice, courage, temperance, and the rest."[326] The opposed vices would be evil. Everything else he regarded as neutral or indifferent. This category included "life, health, pleasure, beauty, strength, wealth, fair fame, and noble birth" as well as their opposites.[327] All that which Cicero regarded as useful Zeno would regard as neutral because it could be used for good or evil.

However, the Stoics did hold that even though many things were not to be categorized as good, one still ought to choose some rather

---

[324] *On Duties* 2.52-85.

[325] Diogenes Laertius, "Zeno" VII.103 in Diogenes Laertius, *Lives of Eminent Philosophers*, trans. R. D. Hicks, The Loeb Classical Library 185 (Cambridge, MA: Harvard UP, 1972), 209.

[326] Diogenes Laertius VII.102, 207.

[327] Diogenes Laertius VII.102, 209.

than others. These were called the preferable. The preferable were those things that "contributed to harmonious living" or somehow contributed to "the life according to nature."[328] For example, wealth or health might be used for good or evil. But if the preferable are used well they could promote living virtuously. Such acts would be regarded as appropriate actions. Cooper observes, "on Stoic theory, all virtuous acts...are also appropriate acts, but not vice versa."[329] That is, for classical Stoicism appropriate actions are broader than virtuous actions. Acting prudently or justly would always be appropriate. Using one's wealth in a way that accords with nature would also be an appropriate action, but would not be a virtuous action. And since, Zeno argued, the only good is the virtuous, using wealth well would be appropriate but not good.

Given Cicero's emphasis on the honorable and his rejection of consequentialist views, one might suspect that he would agree with Zeno and not grant the useful the status of being truly good. He seems to be asserting this when he writes in *On Ends* that "we should believe [the honorable] to be the only good."[330] This passage seems to suggest that Cicero holds that the good and the useful are to be kept distinct.

However, Cicero will reject this position. In fact, later in the same work, he criticizes the Stoic position that completely separates the useful and the good. He claims that the Stoics "leave us with two tasks instead of one – to 'adopt' some things [the preferable], and 'seek' others [the good], rather than including both of them under a single

---

[328] Diogenes Laertius VII.105, 211.

[329] Cooper, 200.

[330] *On Ends* 3.26.

End."[331] His criticism is that in the Stoic view there are two distinct orders of goals. The essential one has the good as its goal. However, there is also a second series of things that are preferable but are not on the same level as the truly good. He takes this position to be incoherent. For Cicero, if something is to be sought, it can only be because it is good. As Colish observes, "The contrast between Cicero's *utile* and the Stoic category of the preferable, which it appears to resemble on the surface, is...striking. The *utile* is in no sense morally neutral for Cicero."[332] That is to say, for Cicero the useful and the honorable are both good. The issue for him is their relationship.

The Useful and the Honorable

Cicero argues that the link between the useful and the honorable is justice. In the previous consideration of the *Dream of Scipio* and *On the Laws* in Chapter 3, we saw that Cicero argued that acting justly is always useful because it is always good. He quoted with approval Socrates cursing "the man who first separated self-interest (*utilitatas*) from justice."[333] He formalizes his point in *On Duties* by expressing it as a syllogism: Everything that is just is useful, and everything that is honorable is just, therefore everything honorable is useful.[334] The minor premise, everything that is honorable is just, expresses Cicero's thesis that to-act honorably, that is appropriately, is to give to everyone what is really due to them.

---

[331] *On Ends* 4.39.

[332] Colish, 148-149.

[333] *On the Laws* 1.33.

[334] *On Duties* 2.10.

The major premise, everything that is just is useful, is less clear, perhaps even paradoxical, but is the essence of Cicero's ethical position. In *On Duties* Cicero will return to the position he developed in the *Dream of Scipio* when he writes that:

> If a man acts violently against someone else in order to secure some advantage for himself, he either considers that he is doing nothing contrary to nature, or else he judges that death, poverty, pain and loss of children, relations or friends are more to be avoided than the doing of an injustice to someone.[335]

Cicero makes use of a dilemma. Such a person, in acting unjustly, either does not think they are acting contrary to nature, or they consider themselves to be acting against nature but to avoid a greater evil, such as death, poverty, or other losses. Regarding the first person, who does not believe they are acting contrary to nature, he would say that "if he thinks that acting violently against other men involves doing nothing contrary to nature – then how can you argue with him? For he takes all the 'human' out of human."[336] Such a person, in Cicero's judgment, has lost their grasp of one of the first principles of human life and conduct. They are acting in a subhuman way.

The other possibility is that "if on the other hand, he thinks that such actions should be avoided, but that death, poverty and pain are far worse, his error is that he counts a failing of body or fortune as more serious than any failing of spirit.[337] In such a case, there is recognition

---

[335] *On Duties* 3.26.

[336] *On Duties* 3.26.

[337] *On Duties* 3.26.

of the basic principles of human conduct. However, there is a failure in judgment. In this case, the failure consists in over valuing physical pain or loss. Once again, as was discussed in Chapter 5, Cicero emphasizes that acting against our nature is never advantageous because it strikes against the very possibility of obtaining our end. His position is that the good is intrinsically desirable.

Moreover, since to do good is always good for us, then it is useful, or to our benefit. On the other hand, "if something is dishonourable, it is never beneficial, not even when you acquire something that you think beneficial." [338] The dishonorable is never useful to us or to anyone because such actions vitiate against the very achievement of the human good. Therefore, Cicero concludes that "all men should have this one object, that the benefit of each individual and the benefit of all together should be the same." [339] So in no case is it useful to act unjustly. Rather, utility is found in acting justly.

Utility thus does have a place in Cicero's ethical position. But, benefits are only truly useful if they promote the true good, which is found in honorable activity. As Walter Nicgorski explains, "utility is allowed by Cicero as a legitimate moral consideration, not a crass pleasure-seeking utility, but utility that is consistent with the overall and true requisites of human nature." [340] The sort of utility Cicero has in mind is not opposed to human nature and virtue. Nicgorski continues by observing, "The useful and the right are one because their context is derived from common sources; they are the names given to different

---

[338] *On Duties* 3.49.

[339] *On Duties* 3.26.

[340] *Paradoxes*, 563.

aspects of the overall requisites of human nature as revealed in its fundamental inclinations."[341] The useful and the right are both evaluated in reference to human nature and the good human life. The useful is only really useful if it promotes fulfillment of that nature and good.

There could only really be a conflict between the useful and the honorable if there could be a true conflict between an individual's good and the common good. As seen in Chapter 5, Cicero rejects this possibility. For him it is not a question of either the common good or my own good. Rather, it is a case of the common good and my good. As Colish observes, this is a consequence of our intrinsically and inescapably social nature, "The reason why they cannot conflict is that man is part of a larger and social and moral whole, which makes radical individualism unacceptable as a basis for ethical action."[342] To be intrinsically sociable means one must consider the common good not just ones own good. Radical individualism presupposes that humans are not intrinsically social beings. Cicero regards this position as untenable.

Cicero's conclusion is that there cannot be a conflict between the honorable and the truly useful, although there can be a conflict between the honorable and the only apparently useful. He considers that great harm has resulted from the error that there can be a conflict between the useful and the honorable:

> Custom has stumbled over this word and strayed from the path, gradually sinking to the point where she has severed honourableness from benefit, decreeing that something can be honourable which is not beneficial, and beneficial which is not

---

[341] *Paradoxes*, 563.

[342] Colish, 150.

honourable. Nothing more destructive than this custom could have been introduced into human life.[343]

This position is destructive because it vitiates the very possibility of living well. According to this belief, one has two choices: seek the honorable or seek the beneficial. Cicero rejects this dichotomy. This declaration once again calls to mind his approval of Socrates's cursing "the man who first separated self-interest (*utilitatas*) from justice."[344]

The Cardinal Virtues Revisited

Cicero clarifies his position on the relationship between the useful and the honorable in the third and final book of *On Duties* by returning to the cardinal virtues. In Book 1 of *On Duties* he considered the relationship of the virtues to the honorable. Now he will consider the cardinal virtues in light of the useful. Cicero will, however, only directly examine three of the cardinal virtues: justice, courage (or magnanimity), and temperance. Omitted will be an explicit consideration of wisdom. This omission is most likely because Cicero considers wisdom to differ significantly from the other cardinal virtues. In *On Ends* he writes that "we do not consider Wisdom to be like seamanship or medicine, but rather like the arts of acting or dancing...its End, being the actual exercise of the art, is contained within the art itself, and is not something extraneous to it."[345] Wisdom involves one's knowing rather than one's external actions. It thus differs from the practical arts but also from the other three cardinal

---

[343] *On Duties* 2.9.

[344] On the *Laws* 1.33. See *On Duties* 2.11.

[345] *On Ends* 3.24.

virtues, which are concerned with social interactions. For these virtues the end is found in external actions. However, knowledge might be acquired justly or unjustly. For example, Cicero regarded it as unjust for one to neglect one's duties in order to pursue esoteric knowledge.[346]

The Useful and Justice

As has been his general procedure, Cicero gives pride of place to justice. He points out that acting justly does not mean to ignore our own well-being. On the contrary, "we are not to neglect benefits to ourselves and surrender them to others when we ourselves need them. Rather, each should attend to what benefits him himself, so far as may be done without injustice to another."[347] Justice is due to all humans, and this includes ourselves. However, our own advantage should never be such as not to render to others what is due to them. To illustrate his point he uses an example from the Stoic philosopher Chrysippus. Cicero comments that "among Chrysippus' many neat remarks was the following: When a man runs in the stadium he ought to struggle and strive with all his might to be victorious, but he ought not to trip his fellow-competitor or to push him over."[348] The point is that it is not unjust to compete with others to obtain some good, but it is unjust to compete in a way that is contrary to the very essence of our social nature. There are limits on what is permissible in seeking our own advantage.

To illustrate the relationship between the useful and the just, Cicero provides some examples of apparent conflict. He considers the

---

[346] *On Duties* 1.69-72.

[347] *On Duties* 3.42.

[348] *On Duties* 3.42.

case of a merchant from Alexandria who arrives with a large supply of corn on the island of Rhodes during a food shortage.[349] The merchant is also aware that several other merchants will also soon be arriving with corn. Ought he not tell the Rhodians of the incoming ships so that he may sell his grain for a higher price? Or ought he rather to reveal that that more ships will soon be arriving even if it will mean less profit for himself? Here there seems to be a conflict between what is beneficial to oneself and the honorable course of action.

Cicero considers as a further example a seller of a house. It would be generally considered useful for the seller to receive the maximum price he or she could obtain for the property. But what if the seller is aware of serious problems with the structure? In his example the house is in poor condition indeed. It is infested with vermin and is disintegrating.[350] Common sense would seem to indicate that these defects should not be emphasized by the seller trumpeting: "I am selling an insanitary house."[351]

Cicero's answer in both cases is that in neither case would the unjust actions be truly useful because they would be contrary to our very nature. What is truly useful would be to profit in a just manner:

> For it is not concealment to be silent about anything, but when you want those in whose interest it would be to know something that you know to remain ignorant, so that you may profit. Who cannot see what this kind of concealment is like,

---

[349] *On Duties* 3.50.

[350] *On Duties* 1.54.

[351] *On Duties* 3.55.

and what sort of man practices it? Certainly not one who is open, straightforward, well bred, just or good.[352]

The act of concealment is not one that flows from a noble character. It is not useful to make oneself unvirtuous. Therefore, such an action is neither honorable or useful.

The Useful and Magnanimity

Cicero next turns to a discussion of courage, or as he describes it, "the greatness and excellence of an outstanding spirit."[353] Cicero will use as his example Regulus, a general during the first Punic War.[354] Regulus was captured and sent back to Rome to transmit the Carthaginians' demand for the return of prisoners. Before being set free, Regulus had to swear that if the Senate failed to agree to the terms, he would return to Carthage. On returning to Rome, he vigorously argued against the peace terms and persuaded the Senate to reject them. Rejecting counsel that he was not obligated to keep his promise, Regulus returned to Carthage and was put to death.

On the surface the honorable and the useful seem to be totally opposed. Regulus may have followed an honorable course of action, but not one that was beneficial or useful to himself or his fellow Romans whom he might have benefited by remaining alive with them. But Cicero will say that although dying, "he was better off than if he had remained at home, a consular but elderly, captive, and

---

[352] *On Duties* 3.57.

[353] *On Duties* 3.96.

[354] *On Duties* 3.99.

foresworn."[355] By breaking his oath Regulus would be striking at the very foundation of the social order. If oaths and promises are not kept, no community can long endure. Breaking his oath would hence not be useful. But, even more importantly for Cicero, Regulus would be acting against his own nature. Therefore, it is both honorable and useful to keep one's oaths, even those made to enemies.

The Useful and Temperance

Finally, and surprisingly briefly, Cicero will turn to the useful in relation to temperance. In this case, the useful or beneficial is the obtaining of pleasure. Cicero will focus on attacking the Epicurean position that pleasure is the highest good. He is aware that Epicurus did not advise overindulgence. Such activity would ultimately produce greater pain than pleasure. His objection, rather, is that the Epicurean view reduces temperance to being only a means to an end, not something worthy choosing for its own sake.

He will argue that this position eliminates the possibility of truly following any of the cardinal virtues, which are the source of the honorable. The 'virtues' are reduced to serving as means to ends rather than being ends in their own right. Wisdom is reduced to a sort of prudence that is "a knowledge that provides pleasures and repels pains."[356] Courage is likewise reinterpreted as "a reasoned method of ignoring death and enduring pain."[357] Even temperance, in this context, is viewed as a means to enhanced pleasure.

---

[355] *On Duties* 3.100.

[356] *On Duties* 3.118.

[357] *On Duties* 3.118.

Although some facsimile of the other three virtues is possible, "justice totters, or rather falls, along with all the virtues that are found in sociability and in the fellowship of the human race."[358] Acting justly requires acting for the good for its own sake. If this does not occur, there is no justice. Hence, Cicero holds that the excessive pursuit of pleasure is not useful because it interferes with the conduct of the virtues which result in the truly beneficial.

Summary

In the second and third books of *On Duties* Cicero draws out some of the implications of his fundamental position that there can never be a true conflict between one's own advantage and what is objectively good or honorable. In particular, he has related the useful to the virtues that constitute a life in accordance with our nature.

We are now ready to make some final comments on Cicero's moral philosophy.

---

[358] *On Duties* 3.118.

CHAPTER VIII
Conclusion

In the introductory chapter we considered why, since the nineteenth century, Cicero has not been taken seriously as a philosopher. We also noted that, although there has been a renewed interest in Cicero's writings in recent years, this interest has been largely found among classicists and political scientists rather than among philosophers. This phenomenon is likely due to a lingering prejudice about Cicero's worthiness to be considered as a serious philosopher.

The objections to Cicero's status as a philosopher appeared to be fourfold. He has been accused of being unoriginal, a mere copyist of earlier philosophers' ideas. Secondly, his philosophical eclecticism seemed to eliminate any claim to logical coherence of his philosophical positions. Thirdly, his allegiance to the skeptical school of philosophy seems to preclude any positive contributions to philosophy. Finally, Cicero has been accused of insincerity, of being a mere propagandist for socially useful beliefs. On this interpretation, rigorous argumentation would take a backseat to patriotic platitudes. Cicero is then dismissed as lacking in philosophical value by those such as Harold Hunt, who contemptuously dismissed Cicero's philosophical works as works in which "pious exhortation takes the place of demonstration."[359]

We have attempted in this book to respond to these charges in a positive fashion, by showing that Cicero does have a cogent, coherent, ethical position. At this stage, it is appropriate to return to the objections raised in the first chapter and briefly offer some final comments regarding them.

In regards to the claim that Cicero is merely a copyist, we have seen that, on the contrary, Cicero does not take any position merely based upon authority. If he follows an earlier philosopher, it is because he finds his argument more compelling. His eclecticism is likewise based upon philosophical reasoning rather than his personal preferences. We have seen that Cicero felt free to criticize and modify the teachings of his predecessors when he thinks they are mistaken. This is especially true in his relation to the Stoic philosophers, in such areas as natural law and the nature of the useful.

Furthermore, Cicero's skepticism is no hindrance to him developing a positive philosophy. As he explains in his *Academics* that, "our arguments [do not] have any purpose other than to draw out or 'formulate' the truth or its closest possible approximation by means of arguing on either side."[360] His skeptical attitude is not one that forbids the search for truth. Instead, he viewed his skeptical method as a means of reaching the troth or that which is more likely to be true.

---

[359] H. A. K. Hunt, *The Humanism of Cicero* (Cambridge: Cambridge UP, 1954), 169.

[360] *Academica* 2.7. Cicero, *On Academic Scepticism*, trans. Charles Brittain (Indianapolis: Hackett, 2006), 6.

Finally, what of the claim that Cicero is not sincere in seeking truth, but only promotes socially useful views that he does not believe in himself? As was discussed in Chapter 1, Cicero's inner convictions and motives are not discoverable with certitude. One can only examine the actual arguments that he makes to see if they are cogent and free from contradictions. Flawed and contradictory arguments suggest sloppiness or lack off sincerity. A coherent line of argumentation does not necessarily prove that an author is sincere, but they do diminish or eliminate the likelihood of an author's deliberate attempt to deceive his readers. In the case of Cicero, this study has attempted to explicate the underlying principles and connecting arguments of Cicero's ethical philosophy and thus show that no glaring inconsistencies are in evidence.

Cicero's Ethical Vision

What is the essence of Ciceronian Ethics? Wood is surely correct in stating that "his unshakable belief in the rational order of the universe and man is perhaps his most basic value, the intellectual underpinning of his other fundamental norms."[361] Cicero's ethics are based fundamentally on a view of human beings as rational agents. From our rational nature, certain principles of action follow. This thesis is expressed in his treatment of natural law.

What sets Cicero's version of natural law apart from many other forms, such as that of Thomas Aquinas, is that Cicero does not presuppose the existence of a God. Rather, Cicero argues from our experience of human life to there being universal principles of conduct

---

[361] Wood, 70.

that make human well being possible. Seeking then to find the most plausible underlying grounds for human nature and life, he concluded to the idea of there being a natural law. The existence of a divine mind then enters as the most plausible account that make natural law possible. Only by acting in accordance with this natural law can we attain the human good. Thus, there can be no real conflict between acting well and seeking our own good.

Cicero's natural law position is developed in *On Duties*. In that work he examines human nature and what activities are in conformity with it. Such actions he will describe as "appropriate actions" or duties. He considered these appropriate actions under the heading of the four cardinal virtues: wisdom, justice, courage, and temperance.

These themes can, of course, be found in other philosophers as well. It would be difficult to discover very many philosophical ideas that are unique to a given philosopher. But Cicero's arguments and vision of the ethical life seem to offer much food for continued analysis and discussion.

BIBLIOGRAPHY

1. Primary Sources

Cicero. *Cicero's Tusculan Disputations, I and Scipio's Dream*. Edited by Frank Ernest Rockwood. 1903. Reprint, Norman: U Oklahoma P, 1966.

---. *On Ends*. Translated by H. Rackham. The Loeb Classical Library 40. Cambridge, MA: Harvard UP, 1914.

---. *Nature of the Gods and Academics*. Translated by H. Rackham. The Loeb Classical Library 268. Cambridge, MA: Harvard UP, 1933.

---. *On Duties*. Translated by Walter Miller. The Loeb Classical Library 30. Cambridge, MA: Harvard UP, 1913.

---. *On the Republic and On the Laws*. Translated by C. W. Keyes. The Loeb Classical Library 213. Cambridge, MA: Harvard UP, 1928.

---. *Letters to Atticus* III. Translated by E. O. Winstedt. The Loeb Classical Library 97. Cambridge, MA: Harvard UP, 1953.

---. *On Academic Scepticism*. Translated by Charles Brittain. Indianapolis: Hackett, 2006.

---. *On Duties*. Translated by E. M. Atkins. Cambridge Texts in the History of Philosophy. Cambridge: Cambridge UP, 1991.

---. *On Moral Ends*. Translated by Raphael Woolf. Cambridge Texts in the History of Philosophy. Cambridge: Cambridge UP, 2001.

---. *On the Commonwealth and On the Laws*. Translated by James E. G. Zetzel. Cambridge Texts in the History of Philosophy. Cambridge: Cambridge UP, 1999.

---. *On Obligations*. Translated by P. G. Walsh. Oxford: Oxford UP, 2000.

--. *On Old Age, On Friendship, On Divination*. Translated by William Armistead Falconer. The Loeb Classical Library 154. Cambridge, MA: Harvard UP, 1923.

---. *Ricerche Sul Testo Del Timeo Ciceroniano*. Edited by Remo Giomini.Rome: Angelo Signorelli, 1967.

---. *The Republic and The Laws*. Translated by Niall Rudd. Oxford: Oxford UP, 1998.

---. *Tusculan Disputations*. Translated by J. E. King. The Loeb Classical Library 141. Cambridge, MA: Harvard UP, 1927.

2. Secondary Sources

Aristotle, *Aristotle's Metaphysics*. Translated by Hippocrates G. Apostle. Grinnell, Iowa: Peripatetic Press, 1966.

Augustine. "De Civitate Dei Contra Paganos Libri XXII." http://www.augustinus.it/latino/cdd/index.htm (accessed July 1, 2021).

---. *The City of God*. Translated by Marcus Dodd. New York: The Modern Library, 1950.

Barlow, J. Jackson. "Cicero on Property and the State." *Cicero's Practical Philosophy.* Edited by Walter Nicgorski, 212-241. South Bend, Ind: University of Notre Dame Press, 2012.

Bruwaene, Martin van den. *La Théologie de Cicéron.* Louvain: Bibliothèque de l'Université, 1937.

Caspar, Timothy W.. *Recovering the Ancient View of Founding: A Commentary on Cicero's De Legibus.* Lanham, MD: Rowman & Littlefield, 2011.

Colish, Marcia L.. *The Stoic Tradition from Antiquity to the Early Middle Ages: I. Stoicism in Classical Latin Literature.* Leiden: Brill, 1985.

Cooper, John M.. *Pursuits of Wisdom: Six Ways of Life in Ancient Philosophy from Socrates to Plotinus.* Princeton: Princeton UP, 2012.

Curd, Patricia, ed. *A Presocratics Reader: Selected Fragments and Testimonia.* Translated by Richard D. McKirahan. Indianapolis: Hackett, 1996.

Davies, J. C. "The Originality of Cicero's Philosophical Works." *Latomus* 30. (Jan-Mar, 1971): 105-119.

Descartes, Rene. *Discourse on Method.* Translated by Donald A. Cress. Indianapolis: Hackett, 1980.

Diogenes Laertius. *Lives of Eminent Philosophers.* Translated by R. D. Hicks. The Loeb Classical Library 184, 185. Cambridge, MA: Harvard UP, 1972.

Douglas, A. E., *Cicero.* Greece and Rome: New Surveys in the Classics 2. Oxford: Oxford UP, 1968.

---. "Cicero the Philosopher." *Cicero*. Edited by T. A. Dorey. London: Routledge & Keegan Paul, 1964. 135-170.

Dyck, Andrew R.. *A Commentary on Cicero, De Legibus*. Ann Arbor: U of Michigan Press, 2004.

---. *A Commentary on Cicero's De Officiis*. Ann Arbor: U of Michigan Press, 1997.

Everitt, Anthony. Cicero: The Life and Times of Rome's Greatest Politician. New York: Random House, 2001.

Ferray, J. L.. "The Statesman and the Law in the Political Philosophy of Cicero." *Justice and Generosity: Studies in Hellenistic Social and Political Philosophy. Proceedings of the Sixth Hellenisticum*. Edited by Andre Laks. Cambridge: Cambridge UP, 1995. 48-73.

Fott, David. "The Politico-Philosophical Character of Cicero's Verdict in *De Natura Deorum*." *Cicero's Practical Philosophy*. Edited by Walter Nicgorski. South Bend, Ind: University of Notre Dame Press, 2012. 152-180.

Glucker, J. P.. "Cicero's Philosophical Affiliations." *The Question of "Eclecticism"*. Edited by J. Dillon and A. A. Long. Berkeley: U of California P, 1988. 34-69.

Görler, W.. "Silencing the Troublemaker: *De Legibus* I.39 and the Continuity of Cicero's Skepticism." *Cicero the Philosopher: Twelve Papers*. Edited by J. G. F. Powell. Oxford: Oxford UP, 1995. 85-113.

Griffin, M. T., Introduction to *Cicero: On Duties*. Translated by M. T. Griffin and E. M. Atkins. Cambridge Texts in the History of Philosophy. Cambridge: Cambridge UP, 1991.

Holton, James E.. "Marcus Tullius Cicero." *History of Political Philosophy* 3rd ed. Edited by Leo Strauss and Joseph Cropsey. Chicago: University of Chicago Press, 1987. 155-175.

Hunt, H. A. K.. *The Humanism of Cicero*. Cambridge: Cambridge UP, 1954.

Kant, Immanuel. *Critique of Pure Reason*. Translated by Norman Kemp. London: Macmillan, 1933.

---. *Grounding for the Metaphysics of Morals*. Translated by Thomas Kingsmill Abbot. London: Longmans, Green and Co., 1895. https://www.gutenberg.org/ebooks/5682 [accessed July 29, 2021]

---. *Grounding for the Metaphysics of Morals*. Translated by James W. Ellington. Indianapolis: Hackett, 1993.

Lewis, C. S.. *The Discarded Image: An Introduction to Medieval and Renaissance Literature*. Cambridge: Cambridge UP, 1964.

Long, A. A.. "Cicero's Plato and Aristotle." *Cicero the Philosopher: Twelve Papers*. Edited by J. G. F. Powell. Oxford: Oxford UP, 1995. 37-61.

MacIntyre, Alasdair. *After Virtue*. Notre Dame: University of Notre Dame Press, 1981.

Mill, John Stuart. *Utilitarianism*. 1863. Reprint, Mineola, NY: Dover, 2007.

MacKendick, Paul L.. *The Philosophical Books of Cicero*. London: Palgrave Macmillan, 1989.

Nagel, Thomas. *Mind and Cosmos: Why the Materialist Neo-Darwinian Conception of Nature is Almost Certainly False.* New York: Oxford UP, 2012.

Nemeth, Charles P. *A Comparative Analysis of Cicero and Aquinas: Nature and the Natural Law.* New York: Bloomsbury, 2017.

Nicgorski, Walter. "Cicero and the Rebirth of Political Philosophy." *Political Science Reviewer.* 8 (1978): 63-101.

---. "Cicero, Citizenship, and the Epicurean Temptation." *Cultivating Citizens: Soulcraft and Citizenship in Contemporary America.* New York: Lexington Books, 2002. 3-28.

---, ed. *Cicero's Practical Philosophy.* South Bend, Ind: University of Notre Dame Press, 2012.

---. *Cicero's Skepticism and His Recovery of Political Philosophy.* New York: Palgrave Macmillan, 2016.

---. "Cicero's Focus: From the Best Regime to the Model Statesman." *Political Theory* 19:2 (May, 1991): 230-251.

---. "Cicero's Paradoxes and His Idea of Utility." *Political Theory* 12:4 (Nov, 1984): 557-578.

---. "Cicero's Socrates: His Assessment of the "Socratic Turn". *Law and Philosophy: The Practice of Theory.* Edited by W. Braithwaite, J. Murley, and R. Stone. vol 1. Athens, Ohio: Ohio UP, 1991. 213-233.

Online Encyclopedia of Philosophy. s.v. "Cicero," http://www.iep.utm.edu/cicero/ [accessed July 1, 2021]

Pease, Arthur Stanley. Introduction. *De Natura Deorum*. 2 vols. Cambridge: Harvard UP, 1955-58.

---. "The Conclusion of Cicero's *De Natura Deorum*." *Transactions and Proceedings of the American Philological Association* 44 (1913): 25-37.

Plato. *The Republic*. Translated by Allan Bloom. New York: Basic Books, 1968.

---. *Timaeus and Critias*. Translated by Desmond Lee. New York: Penguin, 1965.

Porter, Jean. *Nature as Reason: A Thomistic Theory of the Natural Law*. Grand Rapids, MI: William B. Eerdmans, 2005.

Powell, J. G. F.. Explanatory Notes. *The Republic, The Laws*. Oxford: Oxford UP, 1998. 175-242.

---. "Introduction: Cicero's Philosophical Works and their Background." *Cicero the Philosopher: Twelve Papers*. Oxford: Oxford UP, 1995. 1-32.

Poyser, G. F. Introduction. *Cicero: De Re Publica*. Trans G. F. Poyser. Cambridge, MA: Cambridge UP, 1948. 1-37.

Rawson, Elizabeth. "The Interpretation of Cicero's *De Legibus*." *Roman Culture and Society: Collected Papers*. Oxford: Oxford UP, 1991.

Rist, *Epicurus: An Introduction*. New York: Cambridge UP, 1972.

Runia, David T. "Aristotle and Theophrastus Conjoined in the Writings of Cicero." *Cicero's Knowledge of the Peripatos*. Eds. W.

W. Fortenhaugh and P. Steinmetz. Edison, N.J.: Transaction Publishers, 1989. 23-38.

Schofield, Malcolm. "The Fourth Virtue." *Cicero's Practical Philosophy*. Edited by Walter Nicgorski. South Bend, Ind: University of Notre Dame Press, 2012. 43-57.

Simpson, Peter Phillips. "Justice, Consequences, and Cicero." *Vices, Virtues, and Consequences: Essays in Moral and Political Philosophy*. Washington, D.C.: CUA Press, 2001. 75-89.

Strauss, Leo. *Natural Right and History*. Chicago: University of Chicago Press, 1968.

Thomas Aquinas. *Summa Theologiae*. Translated by English Province Dominicans, http://newadvent.org/summa/ (accessed July 1. 2021).

Vlastos, Gregory. *Socrates: Ironist and Moral Philosopher*. Cambridge: Cambridge UP, 1991.

Wood, Neal. *Cicero's Social and Political Thought*. Berkeley: U of California P, 1988.

Woolf, Raphael. *Cicero: The Philosophy of a Roman Sceptic*. New York: Routledge, 2015.

Wright, M. R.. "Cicero on Self-Love and Love of Humanity in *De Finibus* 3." *Cicero the Philosopher: Twelve Papers*. Edited by J.G.F. Powell. Oxford: Oxford UP, 1995. 171-195.

Wynne, J. P. F.. "Cicero," *Skepticism: From Antiquity to the Present*. Edited by Diego Machuca and Baron Reed. New York: Bloomsbury, 2019. 93-101.

---. *Cicero on the Philosophy of Religion: On the Nature of the Gods and On Divination*. New York: Cambridge UP, 2019.

Zetzel, James E. G.. Introduction. *On the Commonwealth and On the Laws*. Cambridge Texts in the History of Philosophy. Cambridge: Cambridge UP, 1999.

Printed in Great Britain
by Amazon

10522392R00089